Love Never Fails You…

Overcoming Life's Trials And Grief

By

Lynn McKenzie

Love Never Fails You
Overcoming Life's Trials And Grief
by Lynn McKenzie

Printed in the United States of America

ISBN 9781613798102

Unless otherwise indicated, Bible quotations are taken from The King James Bible; and The American Standard Version of the Bible.

Contact information for Lynn McKenzie:

Life with Lynnie www.2lynnmc.blogspot.com or
lifewithlynnie@gmail.com

or by mail @

5505 Rhodes Dr. #224, Windsor, ON Canada N8N 2M1

www.xulonpress.com

Dedication

This book is written in honor of God, my Father, who created me, the Holy Spirit, who convicts me and guides me, and my Lord and Savior, Jesus Christ, through whom I have received everlasting life.

So, to God the Father, the Holy Spirit, and of course my Lord Jesus Christ, I thank You, for helping me through the tough times of my life, enabling me to be able to not just survive, but also flourish.

Also, I honor my late husband, Gordon, and my family and friends who have been supportive of me through my grief and other issues that proved to be struggles in my life.

I thank all who helped me, encouraged me, and lifted me up in prayer. Without your loving prayer and support, this book would not be possible. I have elected to not name you here, in case I inadvertently left anyone out. You know who you are. More importantly, God knows who you are. May God bless you for the love and support that you've given me.

My heart's desire is for everyone who is grieving or suffering with life's trials, in need of encouragement or lifting up, to be blessed by reading *Love Never Fails You…*

CONTENTS

Introduction

On my birthday, in 2009, I began to write a blog called *Life with Lynnie* after desiring to do this for a very long time.

Shortly afterward, I began receiving feedback, not just encouraging me, but also letting me know that what I wrote was of importance to others. A ministry, some called it, but in my mind it just reflected me and my life.

Eventually, people began telling me I should either change *Life with Lynnie* into a book format, or consider writing a book. Some who gave feedback were shocked to know that I had no experience as a published author.

For a while, I thought people were just being kind to me, encouraging me to continue writing. However, after several people made the same suggestions and comments, I prayed about the idea of writing a book.

Eventually, I understood that indeed others were interested in what I had to say. So, I prayed for wisdom and guidance.

Once I made the decision to actually publish something, I thought that I would take people's suggestions to heart and compile a book of my blog entries. This way, people who do not use a computer would be able to read my writings.

After giving the idea much prayer and thought, I felt God leading me to keep *Life with Lynnie* just as it was. I decided to sit down and write in a more compact format, suitable for publishing into something anyone can hold in their hands, either on paper or for e-reading.

Your first thought regarding *Love Never Fails You* may be that this story is a compilation of memoirs, meant only to broadcast to the world some of the fiery trials I have experienced in my life, compelling some to feel sorry for me. This is not what I meant this book to be about.

I believe that words can sometimes be cheap; without substance they can be meaningless.

Anyone who has experienced traumatic trials in life will understand that in order for readers to believe what I claim will be of help to them, they will have to know and understand that like them, I have truly suffered in this life.

May God bless you as you read, understand, and accept the love God is showing you through this work He has inspired me to write.

Remember always that Jesus loves you and so do I.

Chapter One

Life, Love, Travel, and Blogs

My husband, Gordon, and I loved to travel. We weren't rich people, but we didn't struggle financially, either. Together, we decided that we wouldn't wait for retirement to see the world, or at least as much of it as we could afford to see. We both felt waiting could bring about lost dreams.

Both of us had parents who had waited until retirement to do some traveling. Unfortunately, neither Gordon's parents nor mine ever got to do the traveling they dreamed of, because both our dads died just before their retirement date. So, we'd talk about where we would like to go, making lists and notes we could refer to whenever we saw a sale that would enable us to travel, somewhere.

Had we been luxury travelers, we would not have travelled as much as we did. We were working people, with limited time off work and limited funds.

We were *budget* travelers.

Whether we drove across various parts of Canada and the US, or whether we flew somewhere, costs were always a factor in our plans. If we didn't want to spend a fortune, we chose to travel somewhere more affordable, from our list of places we wanted to visit. Whenever we knew we would have time off work and the finances to travel somewhere, we made sure that both the location and cost suited our needs.

You see, when Gordon and I married, he assured me we would enjoy life together and that he would show me the world. He did. Show me the world, I mean. Together, even on limited funds, we visited various parts of Canada, the US, the Caribbean, Central America, South America, North Africa, and on several occasions, Europe.

We believed God had finally blessed us, with a loving life. Gordon loved me. I loved him. Together, we enjoyed each day and were fulfilled

By 2008, I had become an avid reader of blogs. Travel blogs. I particularly enjoyed those written by budget travelers, like us. Some were written by people who enjoy camping in recreation vehicles travelling part of the year in their various styles of Recreational Vehicles. Others were full-time RVers, living in their RVs as they travelled throughout various countries.

By 2009, I had decided that when we travelled again, I should create a blog. This way, we would have a more permanent record of our travels, while allowing our family and friends to be able to read about our adventures and know we were enjoying life, safely together.

Originally, I planned to begin my blog writing in the late spring of 2009, even though we weren't due to travel to N. Ireland to attend a family wedding until July that year.

Since I really didn't know *how* to blog, other than I knew I had to write entries, and since I knew nothing about how to organize one, manage one, or even how to publish photos online, I kept putting it off.

In retrospect, it's probably good I didn't begin blogging at that time, because at the end of May, Gordon became ill with rectal bleeding and other issues that hospitalized him for more than a week. His discharge from the hospital in early June surprised us as he still wasn't well.

The hospital physicians performed many invasive and uncomfortable tests, but they never located from where Gordon's body bled out. Anemia was only one of his problems. Even though he relaxed in our comfy apartment, Gordon's outlook took a turn for the worse, as he became increasingly disillusioned with life and our medical system, here in Ontario, Canada. It seemed no matter what we did, we were always up against what I call *The Glass Wall*, where we could see treatment, but not obtain it for him.

Due to Gordon's ill health, we did not travel to N. Ireland in July. We did not attend our family wedding. Missing our trip did nothing to encourage Gordon, but served to be just another disappointment in life, for he loved my Irish relatives and enjoyed visiting with them.

By his birthday at the end of July, Gordon came to the conclusion he would not be healed. He believed his death was certain. Instead of being positive in his thinking, he dropped into an even deeper state of despair. He even stopped praying with me for healing.

Unfortunately, Gordon's insight proved to be correct. He was pronounced dead at twelve-thirty a.m., Saturday, October 10, 2009.

Gordon – Niagara Falls, Ontario, Canada

Gordon – Pisa, Italy

Gordon – Paris, France

Gordon – Haarlem, Netherlands

Gordon – Clapham Common (London), England

Chapter Two

Gordon's Funeral

Gordon – 2007 (Aged 60)

Even though Gordon's health had not been the best, his death overwhelmed me.

Did I cry? No. Not in the beginning. God gave me the composure to live through this without falling apart. He answered my prayer to lift me up and provided for me, so I could get through the horrible ordeal with dignity.

When my husband passed away, one of his relatives, one of my daughters, and our pastor stood at Gordon's bedside with me. I was grateful to have family support, for it was all I could do to remain alive, myself.

The nurse gave us a few minutes with Gordon then we left him at the hospital, for the funeral home was on its way to pick up his body.

Shortly after one a.m., I entered our apartment, alone.

How could I be in a state of shock? But I knew I was. When I climbed into bed and looked over at Gordon's side, it hit me that he would never, *ever* be there with me again.

I am not sure if I actually fell asleep or just plain passed out, for the pain in my heart was severe. My lungs were barely functioning. Each breath was so shallow it surprised me I was breathing at all.

After daylight arrived, I got out of bed, showered, and got ready to leave.

My daughter who had been at the hospital when Gordon died went with me to the funeral home. What a blessing, to not have to do this heartbreaking task alone.

Gordon had asked to be taken to the same mortuary where his parents had been laid out. The patient, kind director and some of his co-workers knew Gordon and his family. I am grateful to the gentleman who assisted me.

He left the room for a few minutes. When he returned, he asked me to pick up the nearby telephone, and speak to the coroner.

My conversation took a little longer than anticipated. We discussed events leading up to Gordon's death then he thanked me for speaking to him.

God was with me, holding me up. His grace allowed me to stay in a state of mind that, to others, appeared to be calm and in control.

Inside, I was dying, even though I walked, talked, and breathed. After all, my husband, the love of my life, had died just hours before. I was grateful for God's grace, for Gordon had truly been my other half.

We in Canada celebrate Thanksgiving the second Monday in October, rather than in November, like our friends in the US. Gordon died on the Saturday of that Thanksgiving weekend and therefore the soonest his funeral could occur would be six days later. We buried my husband on Friday, the sixteenth of October.

It saddens me to think about it, for not only will there be an anniversary of his death on the tenth of October, but also another on the Saturday of Thanksgiving weekend, each year.

In making arrangements, I also had to take into account my brothers, who lived about a three and a half hour drive, away. With them came another complication that made me feel rather sad for I knew that even though they may have wanted to be there, it was an impossible situation.

Unfortunately, with both my brothers being diabetic and having dialysis different days, I realized only one would be able to attend; my younger brother, Glenn, a wheelchair bound double amputee, could not come to celebrate Gordon's life. Compounding my heartbreak, I gave a eulogy for him less than a year later, for he died July 1, 2010,

My older brother and his girlfriend joined other family and friends for Gordon's funeral.

It absolutely amazed me how many people came to give condolences at the visitation. People Gordon knew from work, neighbors, dear friends, and church family kept me busy at Gordon's casket. In fact, at one point, people were lined up even outside the room, to visit with me and view Gordon for their last time.

Still being in a state of shock, I was able to keep my emotions in check. I kept praying that God would give me extra grace to accomplish what I needed to do for Gordon.

At funerals of family and friends, either Gordon or I would speak, and sometimes I would sing. I wanted to do the same for my husband, for I knew this would have made him happy. He loved to hear me sing.

Phew! This was a lot to ask of myself, but when I spoke to my church office staff, it was suggested I come in the day before Gordon's funeral and they would record me singing. That way, if I didn't have the composure I needed, it would be okay. I would have been able to sing for Gordon's funeral. So, that is what I did. I will always be grateful for that suggestion.

Before the service time, Gordon's casket had been placed in my church's fellowship room, in front of the fireplace. Caskets are usually placed in this room for one final visitation prior to a funeral.

My daughter and some of Gordon's family were in attendance, but I stood alone at Gordon's casket.

Once again, I remained busy as people were lined up to view Gordon and speak with me.

One thing I learned from this experience is that I will never, *ever* try to console someone with kind words while their loved one is lying in their casket. I found it very hard emotionally, being heartwarming, while feeling heartbroken, all at the same time.

Most people said kind things, but a couple of people made rather questionable remarks that I felt were hurtful. When this happened, I silently forgave them and then thanked them for their support.

All I say or ever will say to people is that I am very sorry for their loss, and I let them know I am praying for them. Not that I ever did anything different in the past, but I want to ensure I never upset anyone unnecessarily. It's bad enough that the person being spoken to is usually upset or stressed over their loss; there's no need to contribute to any further suffering or heartbreak.

Even so, I realize that people want to feel supportive. And, praise God for that!

When it came time for Gordon's service to begin, people left the fellowship room, allowing me and other family to have a quiet moment with him before his casket was closed.

In the hallway leading to the sanctuary, Gordon's casket was briefly reopened at the request of my daughter's two youngest sons who wanted to have cards they made for Grandpa Gordon included inside with him, so he could know they loved him.

Only by the grace of God was I able to keep my composure throughout the service.

As planned, I gave a eulogy and included a gospel message, no different than I would have done for someone else. Afterwards, the assembled guests listened to the music I had recorded the day before.

The service continued with, a good friend of Gordon's giving another eulogy; his words both heartwarming and humorous. I will be forever grateful to him, for he truly blessed my heart.

Our pastor gave a wonderful, short sermon and spoke about Gordon who he knew well. The hymns were wonderful.

Our sound technician recorded the whole service. I felt blessed that I could send a CD, along with the order of service, Gordon's death notice, and other information to absent family. Plus, I have a copy of the memorial CD that I will keep forever.

After the service, we made our way to the cemetery. Even there, I felt alone, despite the throngs of people in attendance. But, God gave me grace to be able to hold my head high, even though I felt inside like I was dying.

Later, we returned to our church for a reception meal. Originally, I thought I would have to arrange a restaurant for this, but my church family insisted on hosting the event. Their kindness meant a lot less stress and expense for me. What a blessing to not have to make those arrangements! I know the love shown me by our church family would have made Gordon very happy.

In order to understand what happened to Gordon, you need to know about his background and mine.

Chapter Three

Gordon's Earlier Life

Gordon – High School Tenor Drummer,
Walkerville Pipe & Drum Band

Gordon was born and grew up in Windsor, Ontario, Canada. Along with his parents, he lived with his baby brother, five years younger than himself.

While they were truly a middle class family, they were probably better off financially than some, because prior to marrying, Gordon's dad made some very good investments and held mortgages for other people.

Never having the burden of a mortgage themselves, Gordon's family had a pretty good life. Always a late model car in the garage, annual vacations and, of course, the whole family attended church every Sunday.

Gordon's dad usually walked to work, taking a shortcut along the railroad tracks that led from the nearby General Motors plant to the Ford of Canada plant, except in the very worst winter weather.

Gordon had a stay-at-home mom, typical of the era in which they lived. She cooked, cleaned, and took care of the family. She didn't drive and relied on her husband for everything in her life, from handling finances to assisting her with shopping.

She taught her sons to read. This venture began while expecting Gordon. She told us how she used to walk to Willistead Manor, which at the time was being used as a library, and check out books. She would take these volumes into the park and read aloud to Gordon, absolutely sure he could hear her voice.

Believe it or not, it must have worked, for when he began school at Grade 1 level, without attending Kindergarten he already knew how to read. Gordon also came to know Christ at an early age, for he attended Sunday school regularly. Around the time he began to go to school, he became saved and was baptized in Lake Erie.

Gordon became a crossing guard; of course, today schools do not utilize children in this manner. He also raised the flag when asked to do so.

In high school, Gordon proudly played in the Walkerville High School Pipe and Drum Band. He enjoyed being a flourishing tenor drummer, the person you see where the sticks are attached to their hands/wrists and are twirled as they play.

In his youth, Gordon attended several Christian summer camps. As a teenager, he assisted as a leader at many of those same camps, some in Canada and some in the US.

As a member of Youth for Christ, Gordon attended many conferences, both in Windsor and out of town.

Gordon felt loved by his mom, but unfortunately, he didn't always get along with his dad and felt rather unloved by him. He told me he had felt frustrated with life.

As a teen, he once took a girl to see a movie, at the theatre on Ottawa Street, near where they both lived. That evening, he received what he called *the beating of his life*, by his dad. He never truly understood whether it was because the girl wasn't a born-again Christian, or because his dad just never wanted him to go to the movie theatre.

In any case, through his Christian connections, as an older teen, Gordon met his first wife. She didn't live in Windsor.

Marrying young, Gordon moved to the Toronto area. Together, they had a baby, Karen, who died shortly after birth. Naturally, Gordon and his wife were devastated.

It broke my heart hearing him tell me how no family came to support him as he buried Karen, alone. They couldn't afford a proper church funeral service. His wife remained in the hospital, as was typical in the era of the late 1960s, unable to join him for the burial.

Other family members told him that the child was only a baby that God didn't mean for them to have, but their comments only added to his heartbreak. He carried this pain with him, until the day he died.

Later, they had another child.

Their marriage had many problems and eventually ended in separation and later, divorce. When the marriage ended, Gordon had debt beyond belief. He found himself alone, with only the clothes on his back.

For more than a year, Gordon lived without his son. One day, he received a telephone call from his ex-wife, who let him know that if he wanted his son to live with him, he should meet them after work.

Gordon met her at the McDonald's she specified, where he picked up his son, who began living with him. His son had some health issues, but Gordon was elated to be reunited with him.

Gordon experienced many trials in his life, heartbreaking trials that were enough to put anyone *over the edge*. But, he didn't falter.

He trusted God to handle each situation and relied on Him totally.

However, Gordon no longer worshipped at church. He felt uncomfortable at the church where his ex-wife's family participated in ministry, after his marriage fell apart. Whether or not it was truly a case where he wasn't welcome, or whether it was a situation where he felt stressed about being separated, I really cannot say. But, in any case, he did not worship anywhere, at that time.

Gordon's son had a close bond with relatives in Windsor, and his new living situation made spending time with them difficult, so before school started in September, 1980, he made the decision to leave Brampton. Since the marriage break up, he had felt compelled to do what was best for not just him, but also for his son, as any loving parent would. He felt that starting life over again, with family nearby would help his son come to terms with their new life.

This move to Windsor was rather upsetting to me, for Gordon and I had been dating for a while. I knew I would miss him, but realized that he needed to do what he felt in his heart was right.

He and his son moved to Windsor.

Chapter Four

Lynn's Earlier Life

My earlier life wasn't as pleasant as Gordon's had been. While my parents sporadically worshipped at churches of various sorts, depending upon where we lived at the time, they did not consider themselves born-again Christians, often referring to those who spoke about themselves as such as *holy-rollers*!

We lived in Montreal at the time of my birth, being the second child of the marriage which produced a total of four children. Awaiting me was a brother four years older than myself.

My dad worked hard and almost always had more than one job—at times he had three jobs. Despite his limited education, he provided well for his family. I suppose you could say he was a self-made and self-educated man.

Dad endured a hard upbringing during the depression. Life wasn't easy for him and his siblings.

My grandpa couldn't physically or financially provide well for his children during the depression era, mainly due to the fact that my grandma, who had tuberculosis, was hospitalized for many years. So, for a while my dad and some of his siblings lived in an orphanage-type place, where my dad told me hunger never left him.

My mom's family background was somewhat better than my dad's. She was one of thirteen children born to her British immigrant parents; although a few of my mom's siblings died either shortly after birth or as young children.

Mom's dad had been a pipe fitter, who did well for himself, eventually being owner/operator of his own firm that worked on projects like the *Place Ville Marie*, in Montreal. During the depression, while times were tough financially, Mom said they always had food to eat, for they lived on a farm,

Both my parents were in the Canadian Army. I sometimes joke that the only thing worse than having had one parent who was in the army was having both parents with army experience. The reality is that nurturing was almost non-existent, replaced mainly with discipline. One thing is for sure. I learned if you do something, do it right!

My mom joined the Canadian Women's Army Corp (CWAC) and went through her basic training in Kitchener, Ontario. Eventually, mom became stationed Washington, DC, USA, during WW2.

Unfortunately, I have no information regarding what my mom actually did during the war, because being very tight-lipped, she never told us anything about that era; she had made a promise to never divulge information, so she never did. Not even to us, her children.

My dad actually served in the Canadian Army more than once. Due to wanting to help the war effort and always being hungry, my dad kept trying to join the Canadian Army, even before he was old enough to sign up. Try as he might, he just could not manage to accomplish his goal, being well under sixteen years of age at the time.

Eventually, he enlisted, but only for a short time. Once paperwork caught up, proving that my dad was not old enough to be in the army, he was discharged. I actually have all the paperwork showing this to be true. Not giving up, my dad enlisted again, once old enough. Canada decided they would take him!

This time, after basic training, he went overseas and served in England. Dad never mentioned this to me or my siblings, but because he had family in N. Ireland and because his job as a driver allowed him to, he had permission to travel to visit his mom's family. Usually while driving *brass* to and from a location, near where his family lived.

Once the D-Day Invasion of WW2 happened, my dad's whole life changed. Overseas in France and Belgium, he drove a petrol (gasoline) truck. While being highly unlikely that he would be in a position to take prisoners, he did. It happened. My dad received medals for his efforts.

My parents did not meet until after they were both repatriated to Canada. The rest, as they say, is history.

I would like to say that my dad's time spent with family in N. Ireland is a whole other story for another time. But, I will tell you that it is interesting to note that when my Dad first enlisted, he had been signed up without a middle name. As my Granny confirmed later in life, he didn't have one. Still, confusion filled my brain, because my parents had told me I was named after him. By the time the war was over and my dad discharged, he miraculously had obtained a middle name. *Lynn*. Like my name.

There is a story behind this, but I cannot go into detail, at this time. It is enough to say that after my parents' deaths, it became to known to me that I have a sister overseas, born to my dad before my parents met. I suspect I know who my sister is, for I believe I have met her, but I cannot comment on this, at the moment.

I wish I had known about this as a child, for I didn't have a good relationship with my dad. I knew in my heart he didn't love me.

My mom had several miscarriages between births, so by the time my younger siblings came along, it was like having two separate families.

As a child, I did not understand what happened. With every pregnancy, my dad would take a fit. Usually after drinking too much in a non-celebratory manner, he would remind everyone who could hear him, that he didn't want children, at all.

Not knowing my dad was so affected by having a troubled childhood and having a child from a previous relationship that he was unable to have contact with, I thought the problem was me. I thought I was just plain unlovable.

This laid the foundation for me growing up thinking I wasn't worthy of love. It seemed I could do nothing right and felt not good enough, ever.

Thinking my dad would love me more if I were a boy, I found myself climbing trees, playing baseball and *war* with neighborhood friends. I built soap boxes, using my roller skates for wheels.

Only when alone with girlfriends who insisted they wanted to play with dolls did I ever hold any in my hands, for I had no interest in playing with them; I liked stuffed animals, who I knew for sure loved me.

We moved around a lot. In fact, by the time I finished with my high school education, I had attended eight schools. We moved from Montreal, to Detroit where we lived for four years, before returning to Montreal for just over a year. Then, to Clarkson, which is now part of Mississauga, and later we moved to Brampton.

While living in Brampton, something major happened that changed the course of my life. It actually distressed me enough to make me ill.

When I was twelve years old, my mom had become pregnant, once again. Our family physician believed my mom, being thirty-nine years of age, was going through the change of life. He was found to be wrong, once the baby began to kick.

Just as when my mom found herself pregnant before, ending in miscarriage or with the birth of my younger brother Glenn, my dad very angry got drunk. He began verbally assaulting my mom and tried to hit her.

A visiting relative protected Mom, preventing my dad from hurting her. I watched the events unfold as Dad eventually passed out on the hide-a-bed couch where our relative planned to sleep.

Realizing there was nowhere for him to sleep and believing my mom now safe, our visitor left.

Eventually, my dad woke up and the turmoil began again. My mom left the house, but didn't take us with her. Glenn, being sound asleep, was left in my care.

For me, this proved to be a horrible ordeal and an experience I would never forget.

My dad went ballistic, smashing every breakable thing he could find in our kitchen. All the while, screaming at me at the top of his lungs, letting me know how much he hated me and taking out his anger and frustration on me, as I endured his threats. As this was happening, I cleaned up the mess, over and over and over again.

The next morning, as my dad left for work, he took long spikes and sealed both doors and the windows he felt I could escape through. I couldn't phone for help, because he had disconnected the telephone and hidden it away.

Even if I could have tried to phone my mom, I had no idea where she had gone.

Our relative returned to visit and check on us. He removed the spikes from the back door and found me alone with Glenn, who had come down with chicken pox.

We found where dad had hidden the telephone. Our relative showed me how to connect the phone to the wires in the wall, for this being the era before telephone jacks I had to have some basic training in connecting and disconnecting the phone. He also told me where my mom had gone to for safety, for he had spoken to her before coming to see me and Glenn.

Before leaving, he made sure to remind me to disconnect the phone and put it away before my dad arrived home from work. He didn't want me to suffer the consequences that would follow if I didn't take the precautions necessary to protect myself.

The days that followed, for more than a week, I spent caring for Glenn, bathing him and treating his chicken pox with calamine lotion.

Evening after evening, the same things happened, over and over. My dad vented his anger with hatred towards me, assuring me that I just could not be loved, by anyone.

I got through this by thinking about Jesus and knowing that He loved me.

No, I didn't always worship at church at this age, but I knew in my heart that not only did I love Jesus, but that He loved me. I had never forgotten coming to know Him as a child living in Detroit, worshipping at the Methodist church my mom took us to.

Eventually, Glenn grew well enough for us to leave, so our mom took us away. My parents arranged a legal separation. I still have the paperwork in my possession.

We lived away for several weeks. Being summertime, people thought we were on vacation.

After my parents reconciled and my sibling joined us in the world, they sold our home and moved us from Brampton, back to Clarkson, where they owned another house.

Sworn to secrecy about what transpired that summer, I didn't tell anyone for a very long time. My parents did not want anyone to know about their short-term separation, nor the events surrounding the issue. Eventually, the effects of what I had endured while held in captivity made me ill, but this did not matter to anyone, except me.

As a teenager, life wasn't good. In fact, on three occasions I ran away from home.

Without going into much detail, it is enough to say that on one occasion, I lived once again in Brampton, only this time with one of my best friends and her family.

Eventually, I did return to live with my family, but my dad usually tried to avoid me, as I did, him. My mom had long since given up trying to reason with him. Uncomfortable is about the most polite way I can describe my life, but God helped me through every day.

It's funny really, thinking about all this. Even though I was not walking with the Lord, and not worshipping Him at this time, I somehow knew He was there for me, with me.

Every summer while in high school, I took a job. Eventually, I worked full time in an office. My mom and best friend worked there as well, in the factory. This is where I met a fellow I fell for!

We dated and discussed the idea of getting married. One day, I shockingly found out from a fellow worker that the man of my dreams had lied to me. In fact, he was already engaged to someone else. He confirmed to me that his plans were to return to Dublin, Ireland to marry his fiancé. Devastation filled my heart and mind, once more.

Being very stressed over my love life, work life, and family life, I got sick with a terrible headache. For about three days, I tried to sleep, in an effort to have the pain in my head end.

When I didn't improve, my mom took me to the hospital, where the doctor asked if I had taken any illegal drugs; I replied I had not. The emergency room physician examined me, especially around my neck area, where tightness hard as a rock made me feel nauseated from the extreme pain. He gave me something to relax me. I don't think the pill even reached my stomach before it came up and exited my body. As a result, I passed out and remained unconscious.

About a week later, I awoke as a nurse checked my eyes with a flashlight. An EEG and other tests confirmed I had experienced a severe migraine headache. It was recommended I avoid stress.

Upon my return to work, my immediate supervisor expressed anger I had not called *her*. My mom had contacted the usual person regarding my absence, but that person had not notified my supervisor directly. Not wanting any more stress, I quit my job.

In about a week, I began a new job. At my new place of employment, I met my first husband.

I recall thinking how sweet he seemed, that he didn't seem like the kind of person who would ever hurt me the way I had been hurt by other males in my life. At the time, he was twenty-five years old and had never been out on a date. I thought how wonderful it was he was waiting for the right woman!

We didn't know each other long, before we were engaged and married. I thought I'd found someone who truly loved me but it didn't take long to realized my mistake.

Please understand that I do not wish to say anything bad about my first husband, because our divorce was not totally his fault. I realized that I never should have married him in the first place.

When we married, we could not afford a honeymoon, so we just stayed overnight at a local hotel, near the airport. The following day, we returned to his residence, where we planned to live, along with his parents, sister and brother-in-law and their child, plus one of his cousins for a few months, until each could relocate somewhere else. After much consideration and family discussion, it was decided this would become our home. We took the steps necessary to make it ours, legally and financially.

In retrospect, I should have realized we were headed for disaster, but I didn't. How could I have missed it?

Wanting so badly to be loved, I just didn't see the truth. Isn't this the way Satan works?

Satan will make something not quite right seem perfect. He comes to rob, kill, and destroy. If he would only wear that red suit and carry a pitchfork as he is commonly portrayed, it would be simple to realize he is alive and well, doing his best to destroy our lives. But he isn't like that. He just wants to con us into thinking all is well, when it truly is not.

My husband let me know on our wedding night that we could not sleep in the following morning.

He had planned for us to be up early, in order to be able to take his mom somewhere first thing as he had promised her. Meaning, the morning immediately after our wedding night; the morning after marriage had taken place.

Yes, it seemed there were more than just the two of us in our marriage and God wasn't among them. To say the least, we had many problems.

In retrospect, I can see God needed to be with us in the marriage. Neither of us looked to Him for all things in our lives, either.

Counseling didn't happen, for he refused to believe there was any problem. He felt if anyone had a problem it was me and not him. Maybe he was right; maybe not. Only God knows who was correct. However, in the end we drifted apart.

While there's more I could say, I am choosing to not do so, for I do not wish to hurt anyone, including him. Besides, I know there is much he could say about me, too. It takes two to make a marriage and it takes two to break it.

Needless to say, the marriage ended in divorce.

I would be remiss if I didn't say that the best part of my first marriage turned out to be the two beautiful daughters I gave birth to. They are very important people in my life. I praise God for them. Thank you, Lord!

Chapter Five

A Testimony to Love

Lynn – 1980 Before Bus Collision

A s you read at the end of the chapter of Gordon's early life, we were both living in Brampton and were dating, when Gordon's ex-wife called and brought his son to him. Shortly after, he and his son moved to Windsor.

I had made no plans to move to Windsor, even though Gordon kept asking me to. With every telephone call, I felt pressure from him. I knew he loved me and wanted me to once again be close to him, but I just couldn't bring myself to do this. Moving away from Brampton would also affect other people, like my parents, other family and of course, the father of my daughters.

1980 had been quite a year for me. Interest rates were extremely high. I had been interviewed for *Global News*, programming of a television station in Toronto, as I had been collecting names for petition against the high rates. Yup, I got my fifteen minutes of fame!

For those who do not live in Canada, you probably aren't aware that when homeowners obtain a mortgage amortized, for example twenty-five years, the interest rate given is not for the whole twenty-five year period. This is not like a variable rate mortgage; although in some ways, quite often results may be similar.

While the amortization may be twenty-five years, the term may be for ten years, five years, three years or even less. Upon renewal, a homeowner must accept the going rate being charged by the mortgagee, at that time. Payments will be adjusted and the mortgage payments continue at the newly adjusted amount, until another renewal occurs.

In 1980, when I renewed the term of my mortgage, I renewed at a rate of 19.5%. Yes, you read correctly! While I can laugh about this now, I didn't then.

It was upsetting, to say the least. Fear set in.

Knowing that friends of mine who were hoping to build a new home had to qualify at 23%, I became nervous that if I had to renew at that rate, I would probably not be able to afford the payment, I made the decision to sell my townhome.

While my children and I were comfortable, I did not want to risk losing my home and the investment in it that I had originally made. So I made the decision to sell and rent for a while. At least until interest rates dropped to a more normal, stable level, where I could once again feel secure in making an investment.

As a single parent, I felt I needed to keep my family secure, physically and financially. After all, being divorced meant that I had to do things for myself, no longer having a husband to share those responsibilities with.

About the time I first divorced, a friend of mine who had been my supervisor in an office where I worked previously, called me offering me a full-time job with the firm. I gratefully declined. Please don't think that I didn't want to be employed there again, for I truly enjoyed it in the past.

After reviewing the whole situation, I decided my family's best interest would not be served having me work at this job. This became evident when I listed my proposed income and expenses and weighed in the fact that I would have to have my younger daughter in daycare, all day long, Monday through Friday.

Since my children were to spend weekends with their dad, I needed to be able to have quality time with them during the week, when people normally worked. This meant a lot to me, especially since my younger daughter was not yet at the age of entering kindergarten at the time we divorced.

Instead of working one full-time job, I decided to work three part-time jobs.

My ex-husband and I agreed to continue operating a small accounting business as we had done for several years. So, even after our divorce I was able to work from home, doing bookkeeping, after my children were asleep.

In addition, I had been working part-time as a manager for a cosmetics firm, doing home parties, hiring people and training them. I had taken skin care and make-up artistry courses and found I had talent in doing make-up for women, which made this business even more financially rewarding.

Especially in summer season, I found myself extremely busy, doing make-up for bridal parties just about every Saturday when my children were with my ex-husband. I truly did not want to give up doing this.

Even so, working at both the cosmetics and the bookkeeping businesses didn't allow me to have enough *guaranteed* income with which to support my family. So, I became licensed to drive a school bus.

It seemed like a perfect job for me. After all, I would be working while my children were in school, once my younger daughter began kindergarten; until then, my employer allowed me to bring her with me, on the bus.

Being able to be with my children when they were off during school breaks and during the summer was the best part! It worked perfectly, from 1978, both for my family needs and my finances; at least until September 30, 1980.

While what I am about to write about is truly a story for another time, but because the after effects of what happened changed my life, I feel compelled to at least let you know what happened. I believe this is truly a testimony to God's goodness.

September 30, 1980 began no differently than any other day. My elder daughter attended grade three at school, while my younger daughter attended kindergarten, mornings only.

As per the norm every afternoon, she came with me on the bus, which I had permission to park at Bramalea City Centre's parking lot. Together, we drove to Malton, a part of Mississauga, where I picked up children and dropped them off, near where they lived.

After dropping off my final group of fifty-three children, I made my way north on Airport Road and turned west onto Clark Blvd., heading back to Bramalea City Centre to park my bus and pick up my car.

Something different happened that afternoon. Normally, my daughter would nap on the seat immediately behind me. On this fateful day, she didn't fall asleep, but found herself awake and rather bored, too short to be able to see out the window beside her.

My four year old asked me if she could stand up and look out the window. I let her know that I thought she should remain seated, being safer for her. She promised that she wouldn't run around the bus *"like the kids do"*, so I agreed to allow her to stand up and look out, as long as she held onto the bar in front of her seat, separating the driver and passenger areas.

I signaled my lane change and moved into the curb lane, because just past Walker St. I would be approaching a set of railway tracks that I would have to stop at, doing the usual routine of opening the door and checking to ensure no train would bear down on us. But, we never made it to the railway tracks.

To my right, the cab part of a tractor-trailer approached the stop sign on Walker St. rather quickly. When the truck did not appear to slow down to stop, I did my best to stop the bus.

I geared down, slamming on the brakes in an effort to avoid collision. The last thing I said to my daughter was, "Hold on and don't let go!" before praying for her, asking God to protect her.

Now, I must tell you that at this time, I didn't consider myself a born-again Christian, for I really didn't worship God at that time, anywhere. And, even when I had gone to church, a Bible-believing, Bible-preaching church would not have been where I would have gone to worship.

Even so, I prayed, envisioning Jesus while doing so.

It will take longer for me to write and describe what happened than it did for the actual collision to occur, for the whole thing happened in a matter of seconds.

The truck did not come to a halt at the stop sign. As he entered the intersection, he hit the front part of my bus. As he tore off the front of my bus, he turned his head to look over at me. Our eyes met for a split second. He looked shocked!

Upon impact, everything seemed to be in slow motion. In reality, it didn't happen this way.

Having a steering wheel to hold onto, I thought I'd be okay. But, I couldn't hold on. My head cracked the windshield. My chest broke the steering wheel. Thrown around like a rag doll, I was eventually thrown out of my seat onto the floor of the bus, after bashing my toes in the process and my knee on the gear shift. My head/neck hit on the pole behind me, just before I landed twisted up like a pretzel on my right side and shoulder, with my lap belt still done up around me.

In retrospect, I am glad I wore my seatbelt, even if only a lap belt, for it stopped me from being thrown out of the bus door's window.

Disoriented, I managed to get my wits about me, twisted myself around and tried to undo my seatbelt. It took every bit of energy I had to push hard enough on the button to unlock the belt, to open it. After several tries, it happened.

By then, the bus was on fire. People who had witnessed the collision were at the door, trying desperately to open it.

Managing to get up, I unlocked the door and the witnesses pushed it open.

Not hearing a sound from my tiny daughter, I envisioned that she had been thrown out of the vehicle. My four and a half year old baby girl did not have the strength needed to hold that bar tight enough to secure her; I knew this in my heart and mind. After all, I wore a seatbelt and had a steering wheel to grasp and couldn't hold on, to secure my own body from injury; I believed that she could not have done as I had directed her to do. My second thought was that she had been thrown out of the bus, probably dead.

I turned to where I had last known her to be standing.

There she stood. Silently staring ahead, not moving. Her tiny hands still firmly grasping the foam-covered bar she had been gripping before impact.

I had to peel her fingers off the foam, one by one.

Just as I finished freeing my child's hands, a witness who had entered the bus grabbed me and helped me get out. Another man did the same for my daughter.

Before the ambulance arrived to take us to the hospital, we were taken to a car owned by one of our helpers.

One angel of mercy held my little one in his arms, sheltering her from the sight of the burning bus that still held her favorite doll. Another man, face-to-face with me placed his arms around me, preventing me from seeing the horror of the bus or the hardworking, brave firemen extinguishing the flames.

These men told me that they witnessed a miracle. Upon impact, they had seen my daughter's body swing up towards the ceiling of the bus and come crashing down again, hitting the bar she had been holding onto. The only injury she suffered that we were aware of at the time was bruising just a bit lower than her throat. Later, I was informed at the hospital, that had she been an inch or two shorter, she would have probably been killed. If she had died, I don't truly know what I would have done. I feel confident enough to say that God would have carried me through yet another of life's trials, but I am grateful I didn't have to endure one of that nature.

By the time the ambulance arrived, I could no longer hold my head up. I could not move my chin from where it lay on my chest without using my hands to lift it. My injuries were multiple, although none were life-threatening. Dislocated shoulders, whiplash, a bashed-up and cut knee, broken toes and more, ensured my pain would be around for some time.

I will write about this collision and the resulting trauma in more detail at a later date.

I still praise God that He chose to spare the life of my baby girl. No one will *ever* be able to convince me that any reason existed for my precious daughter to have been able to survive. She had no earthly protection.

I knew then and will always declare that it could only have been the loving arms of Jesus that protected her, saving her from death that day.

Thank You, Lord! I am and will always be eternally grateful.

Chapter Six

Windsor, the First Time

Since the hospital couldn't reach my parents, they eventually contacted my ex-husband, who gave me a ride home from hospital. He took both my daughters to his house so I could rest.

My parents came to see me later that evening. My dad worked for the Toronto Transit Commission (TTC) at the time, so he had an interest in knowing what happened. My mom's concern appeared to be more for her than for me.

On the day of the bus collision, Mom had taken their telephone off the hook while she had been resting. It explained why when the hospital tried to reach her, they couldn't.

To me, this was not of great concern. However, immediately upon arriving with my dad, mom quietly asked me to not let dad know *why* they could not be reached. Truly, I felt badly for her, for even after all their married years she still lived in a mode of fear.

Every evening, Gordon would telephone me, or I would call him. When he heard of the collision, he told me of his concern for me and my daughter. He felt compelled to come see me, but I insisted he not make the trip, because I believed I would feel better, soon.

Much to my dismay, I didn't feel better, soon.

As I mentioned previously, if I were to write about the condition of my health and about the anxiety I experienced, I would be writing a book solely about this collision. Since this is not my intention at this time, it is enough to say that I suffered, for a very long time.

After a couple of weeks, Gordon came to visit me. He wore a shocked expression when he first saw me and asked me why I hadn't told him how badly I had been hurt. I replied that I thought I would feel better and hadn't wanted him to be unnecessarily concerned.

Well, he was upset. In fact, he was angry with both the driver of the truck for causing the collision and with me, for not speaking up about my injuries.

Prior to the collision, I had been already half packed to move out of my townhome into a rental unit. Gordon insisted on finishing up my preparations. At this time, there was only about a few weeks before the closing was due to happen.

Gordon insisted that I could not take care of myself. He returned to Windsor and made plans to relocate me, so he could care for me during my recovery.

This, my friends, is the story of how I came to live in Windsor. Truly, my mind was in turmoil, for I knew that no one would be happy about this but Gordon. Well, given my health, not even him.

When we speak about love, we know that the Bible tells us in 1 Corinthians 13:4, *"Love is patient. Love is kind. Love isn't jealous. It doesn't sing its own praises. It isn't arrogant."* This described Gordon, although I didn't realize it at the time, for I hadn't been walking with God and hadn't been reading my Bible, to understand this.

Even so, I knew Gordon loved me.

A bowl of cherries, didn't describe my life. My ex-husband didn't like the idea of his children moving to Windsor with me.

Gordon transported my children to and from London, Ontario, every weekend for more than half a year, until I became well enough to take over their transport.

My health didn't improve much, nor did my emotional state. After attending court, where the truck driver received a fifty-six dollar fine and some points against his license for being convicted of failing to stop, my emotional state worsened.

You see, the driver approached me and a friend of mine who was there for my support, after his court conviction. He admitted that he hadn't seen the stop sign, nor my bus or any other traffic in the intersection, including the other school bus that he narrowly missed hitting after he struck mine.

Shocked, I asked him how he could miss a forty-four foot long yellow and black thing. After all, that's why they paint school buses those colors.

He admitted to us that he had, in fact, passed out and had only awoken upon impact.

Ah! The answer to the question that had haunted me ever since the collision: When his eyes met mine upon impact, why did he look surprised? I had my answer.

Before court, I felt physically and emotionally awful. I had felt like I had been raped or better yet, like I had died that fateful day, with some new unknown person invading and occupying my body. After court, I became even worse.

Well, that's enough of that, except to say that I suffered in agony, with physical treatment lasting many years. In fact, I am still recovering at this time.

My suffering wasn't the only suffering that continued. My children suffered. Gordon suffered. Everyone suffered.

Not only did I feel like I no longer existed, but Gordon felt like I disappeared, too. The old me died that fateful day; a newer, broken me replaced her. He took good care of me, but things were different.

Up to this time, Gordon had been a casual drinker, but after the collision he began drinking more heavily. His frustration with the driver of the truck that hit me became obvious, for not only was he drinking on a regular basis, but he regularly spoke of his anger towards him.

Even though we continued our relationship, it changed to on-again, off-again, rather than a firmly committed one.

After a few years, Gordon quit drinking. Even so, being still single and living on my own with my children, I just could not see myself committing to a permanent relationship with him, in marriage.

My daughters missed seeing him visit and would phone him behind my back. They encouraged us to restore our relationship. Eventually, this happened.

Then something occurred that really shook my life. My ex-husband announced his upcoming second marriage. While not being upsetting on a personal level for me, for I had long since known that he never loved me, my children were greatly affected by this news.

Then, another horrible ordeal happened to me around this same time. Workers' Compensation Board doctors had declared me healthy enough to do any kind of work, even though I knew in my heart they were wrong. Consequently, even though I had begun working again, I suffered a subsequent back injury.

Feeling my life once again falling apart, my emotional state suffered. With my children emotionally upset about their dad remarrying, I felt that even though I needed to be totally there for them, I just couldn't be.

Life became a living hell, to say the least. I cried out to God, "*Where are You?*" knowing full-well that He never left my side, aware that He carried me through yet another heartbreaking trial of life.

Just the thought of having more contact with Workers' Compensation Board gave me a sense of despair, after what I had been through with them since the bus collision.

Eventually, my children were so upset over their rapidly changing lives that my older daughter decided she wanted what she thought would be a better life, by going to live with her dad.

Thinking about having my daughters separated from each other made me very unhappy, so I made a decision that drastically affected everyone's life. I said that if one daughter went to live with Dad, then the other would have to go, too. This way, they would have each other if things didn't work out the way they hoped.

Well, things didn't work out the way they hoped that summer. After only a couple of weeks, they were asking to move back again. I insisted that they couldn't play one parent against the other and let them know that if they wanted to move home, they could do so, but not until towards the end of summer vacation. This way, there would be no going and coming at will.

By the time they returned to Windsor, Gordon's and my relationship had resumed.

Even so, turmoil like this didn't end, but continued. Not having recovered fully, I still had health problems and developed more, eventually enduring many surgeries.

A few years later, life fell apart once again. My elder daughter returned to living with her dad. Not long after, she met a fellow and eventually moved to Ottawa, where they were married.

My younger daughter followed suit. She went to live with her dad, too.

My daughter in Ottawa and I talked by phone, regularly. She assured me that even though her younger sister, being a teenager, didn't tell me she needed me, she really did.

About this time, a relative living in the suburban Toronto area needed a better place to live. I called a realtor friend of mine, who had previously lived in Windsor, whose spouse worked for a property management company.

When I explained the reason for my call, they told me they were moving back to Windsor and my relative could have their apartment, in downtown Brampton, across from City Hall, and next to Gage Park.

Together, we I went to see the apartment. It turned out to be better than we expected, so an application to sub-let followed.

Unfortunately, due to my relative not having secure full-time employment, the property manager would not approve the application; they wanted me to put the lease in my name, making me responsible, since they had known me for several years and I had been the person with the stable working history. So, in an effort to help, I did this.

After this, my relative continuously encouraged me to leave Windsor and share the apartment. I gave it serious thought and made the decision to give it a try, because if my younger daughter truly needed me, then I needed to be there for her.

In the meantime, my relative changed her mind about living in the apartment. This meant I had an empty apartment I had to pay for, in addition to paying the expenses on a home I owned in Windsor.

Even though Gordon felt unhappy about me leaving Windsor, he agreed that at least on a temporary basis of a year or so, we could continue a long-distance relationship. He remained in Windsor. I sold my home and moved to Brampton.

Well, even though he didn't want me to leave Windsor, Gordon helped me move all my belongings, once again!

It never ceased to amaze me how much he truly loved me. Unhappy about me leaving Windsor, he understood my need to go and stood by my decision.

Of course, God orchestrated the whole scenario. If He hadn't been in control, providing for the needs of myself and everyone else concerned, none of this would ever have happened. And, Gordon would never have loved me enough to let me go.

Chapter Seven

Brampton, Once Again

Before moving back to Brampton, my Mom, siblings and even some cousins had told me how happy they were that I was moving *home*.

This meant a lot to me, because during the time I had lived in Windsor, my parents and I had a falling out and I was anxious to improve our relationship.

Our relationship had been reborn just two weeks before my Dad died. He had been on a waiting list for more than six years, to have bypass heart surgery.

Unfortunately, by the time his scheduled heart surgery was imminent my dad had unknowingly developed colon cancer. While in the emergency room at a Toronto hospital, he had his first heart attack. The second one killed him.

After waiting so very long for his much-needed surgery, some Toronto newspapers went wild over my dad's story. Such uproar occurred over our good, but broken socialized medical healthcare system, that more than one article had prominent placement on the front pages.

It's too bad that my Dad's fifteen minutes of fame came after his death. Still, many people were helped by what happened to him, because after the ruckus, more centers in our province opened up to accommodate the lengthy list of people requiring heart surgery.

In any case, I thought my relatives were happy that I had returned to Brampton to live. Unfortunately, I didn't feel it turned out to be the case.

During the two years I lived back in Brampton, I rarely saw any relatives at all, unless I went to visit them.

Even though my mom drove to Brampton a couple of times per week to play bingo at a location only six minutes from my residence, she only visited me at my apartment, twice in the two years I lived there. My siblings came only on rare occasion.

For a time, my younger daughter came to live with me, but being a teenager, this didn't last long.

She went to visit her sister in Ottawa. The visit seemed to go on and on, until eventually, I got a call from her, letting me know she met a fellow and didn't plan to return to Brampton.

I began to wonder why I had moved back to that area, after all! Again, I wondered about God's plan for my life. Once again, I felt alone, unwanted, and unloved.

Something *was* very different in my life, though. Unlike many years in the past, where I had rarely worshipped God at church, I had begun to once again to honor Him. Every Sunday, I found myself worshipping somewhere, anywhere. I felt compelled to do this.

How did this change happen? What caused this transformation?

While unpacking in my new apartment in Brampton, I had found my old New Testament Bible that I had been given in fifth grade by the Gideons.

When I came across this tiny Bible, fond memories flashed in my mind's eye. I recalled being ten years old, sitting on my parents' porch, reading this New Testament. I recalled signing it. I recalled the comforting feeling I had while reading it.

I began once again to read this very same Bible. At some point in this experience, lying on my bed reading, an emotion came over me that I had never before felt; sadness. God-related sadness overwhelmed me. I began to cry.

While I had always loved and trusted in Jesus, ever since being a child singing in that pre-junior choir at the Methodist church in Detroit, I realized how very far from God I had gotten. No, I hadn't robbed banks or killed anyone, but I recognized that I had grown very far apart from God.

Even though I had physical problems, I got onto my knees at the side of my bed and prayed to God. I confessed how badly I felt about how I had not always walked with Him in my life. I told Jesus that I *was totally and completely sorry* that I had ever hurt Him, for I truly loved Him. I repented and turned back to God.

Before my younger daughter had left for Ottawa, I had prayed for her; she had begun worshipping at the Salvation Army Citadel in Bramalea and had dedicated her life to Jesus, which had been one reason I had begun to worship Him, again. This is where we together worshipped, until she left for Ottawa.

For a while, I continued worshipping at the Salvation Army. However, not wanting to be reminded of the absence of my daughter every Sunday at that church, I began worshipping at other churches, including a United Church close to where I lived.

God answered my prayer. He began to show me what His plan was for my life and what I was doing in Brampton.

God's plan for me came into view, right in front of my eyes, through my work.

As His plan unfolded, I found myself feeling rather stressed, for He had once again opened the door to pain. Pain that earlier in my life I could not face and deal with.

I had originally become a licensed realtor in 1988. In 1992, when I moved back to Brampton, I transferred with Canada Trust Realty, the brokerage firm I had been employed with, in Windsor.

Brampton had changed much since I had left there in 1980. In 1992, we realtors did inspections after our Monday morning meetings. In Brampton, they called it *going on caravan*. This gave me an opportunity to get to know housing, demographics and my fellow realtors while driving about this area that had changed immensely during my absence.

We usually took turns driving on caravan. This one particular day, as a passenger who did not have the list of the properties we were going to see, I just followed my co-workers' lead.

The driver pulled up in front of the matrimonial home I owned prior to being divorced in 1978. My heart beat in my throat as I exited the vehicle.

At first, I didn't say anything to anyone. It took away my breath, entering this house, revisiting and having memories arise, once again.

Some things had changed; some things had remained the same. Room by room I went, being reminded of both good and not-so-good memories. By the time we left, my heart broke.

I wanted to cry, but managed to hold back the tears. Afterward, I told one of my closest coworkers what had upset me. No one else knew, but God knew.

God used this caravan experience to re-open the wound that had not yet healed, even after all these years.

Praying to Him on a regular basis, confessing to Him, and asking Him to help heal my life, little by little, I felt His healing warmth as I recommitted my life to Him.

God made it clear to me that I had to forgive my ex-husband; and, myself.

While I didn't outright make an effort to contact my ex-husband, a time arose when I had an opportunity to speak with him when our paths crossed. I decided to let him know I forgave him for his part in our divorce and prayed he would forgive me, for my part.

Doing this must have caught him off-guard, for he just looked at me as if I was a crazy person. He silently turned and went to rejoin his wife.

Even so, I'm glad I did this, for I knew that I had to have truly forgiven him in order to have done this. It also meant that I had come to terms with the whole ordeal.

The rest, as they say, would be up to God.

Once this trial ended, I felt I could take a deep breath and get on with my life, but God had other plans.

The house I had lived in from 1962-1964 had been listed for sale. My first thought upon seeing my childhood home on the market, was *here we go, again*! Another trial to work through! And, it proved itself to be true.

Upon hearing of an open house scheduled, I called my mom and asked if she would like to come through with me. Instead of giving a yes or no answer, she shocked me with her reply. "*What home are you talking about? I never lived in Brampton!*"

Mom's response nearly blew me away! How could she not recall living there?! Didn't she recall the heartbreaking situation that occurred, causing me physical and emotional pain, scarring me for life?

Once I reminded her about the situation, she changed her mind about recalling our life there and said, "*Oh, that house! No. I don't want to see it.*"

Not long after we hung up from our telephone conversation, a relative let me know she'd like to see the home with me.

Together, we entered the open house; separately, we looked in each room. Much like when I went through my last matrimonial home, my heart felt heavy.

Room by room, I walked through it and felt grateful the house was vacant with very little furniture left in it. This made it easier to recall how it looked when I had lived there thirty years earlier.

Memories both good and bad flashed through my mind. At one point, I could hardly go further, for tears had overcome me.

In my parents' bedroom, I recalled finding Christmas presents by accident one year, when my mom had forgotten they were there and had asked me to bring something to her from in her closet.

Visions ran through my mind of one of my brothers threatening and chasing me as we ran through the house. Eventually, I had arrived in my bedroom and moved my dresser in front of the door to slow him down. He managed to enter my room. Laughing, I climbed onto the windowsill and told him if he came any closer, I would jump. As he lunged towards me, I jumped!

Believe me, there were tears in my eyes, from the pain of landing in the backyard. I never thought he would hurt me, as I thought the whole episode was one of fun and not truly serious. No matter the case, it is a memory I will never forget!

Spending time in my old bedroom brought that and other memories flashing back in my mind.

While paint colors had changed, it mostly still looked the same. The pine-paneled wainscoted walls my dad had installed in the family room were still in place. I even opened a hiding place he had built in, not being sure if anyone else knew of its whereabouts.

One thing was changed. The telephone jack in the upper hallway, where I had once sat to connect up and disconnect the phone my dad had hidden away from me had been replaced by the newer type where you just plugged in the phone.

I stood at the top of the landing, looking down those few steps, recalling in my mind's eye that fateful night that had never left my memory. I walked towards the side door that had once been nailed shut, so I couldn't leave.

Yet, I had a comforting thought, too. My dad used to hang his money belt at that side door closet, when he had been a milkman, prior to working for the Toronto Transit Commission. Why I found this comforting, I'm not really sure. But, it was.

Rather melancholy, it was the last memory I have of my childhood, there.

Over the years, I have driven by many times. In fact, every time I find myself in Brampton, I make time to drive by. Most often, while doing so, I wish I could somehow erase the bad memories of the past.

But, the past *is* the past. Nothing *can* make it different. The only thing we can change is the way we feel about it.

This is where God comes into the equation. Without Him, I could not have dealt with going through my childhood home filled with memories of trauma that broke my life in so many ways.

He helped me deal with the circumstances that happened there. He helped me forgive the painful trauma that played such a large part in affecting my life. It's never easy to do, but forgiveness is absolutely necessary.

But, He did this, for me. Why? Because, He loved me... and He still does.

The whole time I lived in Brampton, Gordon kept calling and from time to time, visited. Once, he brought with him his son and his son's family. Yes, people could and did call him Grandpa Gordon!

Wanting to make this visit almost like a family reunion, I invited my daughters, who were both living in Ottawa, at the time. They came to Brampton and stayed with their dad and his family.

However, what makes this reunion of sorts so special is the fact that my mom actually came to my apartment that day to join us. In fact, I have a photo of her, Gordon and his family, plus my children and family. Yes, I am a grandma!

What a great memory to have! Every time I look at that photo, I find myself wishing that life could be that good, every day.

For sure, Gordon thought along the same lines. He called me regularly, never letting me forget that he loved me. Over and over, requesting I return to Windsor.

He never gave up asking me to marry him. At the time, I just couldn't bring myself to do this, even if I did love him. And, I did.

On one occasion, he called and let me know he was driving from Windsor to Brampton to take me out to dinner. When he arrived, several hours later, he told me he had a reservation for us at a nearby Vesuvio's Italian restaurant.

Upon entering the restaurant, we were seated in a rather secluded section. A violinist began playing just for us. I thought, *how romantic*!

A waiter came and took our order. Since neither of us drank alcoholic beverages, we were served lovely goblets of water.

Just as I lifted my glass to take a sip, several waiters gathered around, behind Gordon. Everyone looked at me, smiling from ear to ear. Forgive me, but at this time, I still hadn't clued in to what was happening.

Feeling rather odd, I took a sip of my water. As I replaced my glass to where it had once stood, I noticed something in it.

Smiles continued all around.

By now, you've probably guessed Gordon planned to propose to me. Only after I saw the engagement ring, did I realize this. The diamond solitaire sparkled brightly in the softly lit room. It was enticing. My heart skipped a beat. Yet, at the same time, I felt sad.

Over and over, in the past, he had proposed marriage to me. Over and over, I refused, letting him know I loved him, but just could not marry him. Always, he would let me know that he would never again ask me to marry him. But he always did.

And, on this special night, Gordon once again asked me to marry him.

When I realized the reason why all the staff crowded around, hoping to see me joyfully accept Gordon's proposal, I began to panic. How could I let him down? Embarrass him in front of all those people.

I smiled and quietly whispered to Gordon that I would need to think about how to answer. Truly, I don't think he understood what I meant.

Gordon asked me to wear the ring, until I made up my mind.

Meanwhile, everyone standing around began to look disappointed, because I hadn't jumped up, hugging the love of my life and committing to him.

Not wanting to make this any worse than it already looked, he took the ring and I let him place it on my finger. Not on the finger where engagement rings would normally be placed, but rather, on another finger.

Once we were alone, I realized Gordon had set this whole thing up so that he would have a better chance of me saying yes to his proposal. He knew I loved him. He loved me.

So why not do this? Well, all my leftover garbage from the past stopped me.

After we left the restaurant, we had a serious talk. I removed the ring from my finger and asked Gordon to return it to the store and get a refund.

He did this.

However, it didn't stop him from calling me, pleading with me to reconsider and marry him. Eventually, I gave in, at least partially.

Both my daughters were living in Ottawa, claiming they would never return to Brampton. Once again, I wondered why I was staying there, all alone. Especially knowing the love of my life lived several hours away.

During one conversation, Gordon convinced me to at least return to live in Windsor. In fact, he wanted me to purchase the property next door to the one he owned, so that we could be neighbors.

Go ahead. Laugh. I did.

I made it plain that I certainly wouldn't purchase a house next door to his. This would be fine as long as our relationship remained again on, but what if our relationship became, once again, off?

In the end, Gordon decided to purchase the property to use for student rental. However, since it needed some work, he suggested rather than me renting somewhere else to live until I could purchase a home for myself, I should live in it, until he was able to prepare it for rental use.

I agreed. We made plans to once again move me to Windsor. This happened over the Christmas week, 1993.

I didn't plan to give up my apartment until the end of January 1994. This allowed me enough time to go back and clean everything to make it spic and span, before returning the keys to the unit.

Even though life had truly been a mixed up mess, I could see God in the midst of it. He seemed to have everything under control, once again. I needed to just trust Him.

He promised to never leave us, nor forsake us, that He would be with us always, even 'til the end of the age. So, how could we lose? We couldn't, as long as we remained trusting in Him and His plan for our lives.

Chapter Eight

Windsor, Once Again

Things went as planned. I moved into Gordon's newly acquired investment property, where I planned to stay only until I could purchase a home for myself, once again.

I gave Gordon my Brampton apartment keys, so he could stay there when he took his course, in Toronto. He felt he needed something to do while on lay-off from his job in Windsor and had decided to take the Mortgage Broker's course. We both thought this potential career change would complement my real estate career, as we could work together on some deals.

Then, fate struck, again. In retrospect, I can see that it wasn't really fate, but rather, God taking control, once again.

While in Windsor for the weekend, Gordon opened important mail from General Motors of Canada. He had been hired at the GM Diesel Locomotive plant, in London, Ontario, scheduled to begin working the very next week.

Gordon completed the course classroom time, but never wrote the final exam for the mortgage broker's license in Toronto. Instead, he moved to London to work as an electrician, wiring diesel locomotives, where he remained for about a year and a half.

Over the course of that time, I lived in his rental property that he wanted to renovate. He hadn't been able to do this while living so far away.

Gordon asked me to not leave, claiming he didn't want the property vacant. He knew I wanted to purchase a home once again, but asked me to stay living in his newly acquired investment and take care of it and the house next door that he had been living in while sharing part of the premises with university students.

I did.

This living arrangement continued until Gordon's recall to the GM Windsor Transmission Plant. Eventually, he gave up his position in London and returned to Windsor to live.

One thing I need to say is that once I had relocated to Windsor, both my daughters surprised me by deciding they wanted to return to there as well.

First, my younger daughter and her husband moved into town. Then, her sister did, too, along with her family.

About the time Gordon returned to Windsor from London, my daughters lived in the upper units of a four-unit building, across the hall from each other.

A terrible thing happened, late one night. Or maybe I should say early one morning.

A knock came to my daughter's door, after one a.m.

With her husband in the washroom, their toddler son asleep in his room, and thinking it was her sister at the door, she opened the door.

Four young men shoved the door, knocking her over.

One held a baseball bat to her head, threatening to kill her if she screamed or tried to leave. This same person threatened to kill my grandson if he didn't stop crying, after he awoke due to the noise of the intrusion.

A second one grabbed her phone, cutting the wire with a knife; this person eventually took the phone with them, as they left.

A third person found her husband in the washroom and beat him, demanding repeatedly to know where their money and valuables were located.

The fourth and last fellow ransacked their apartment, eventually leaving with all their jewelry, including their wedding rings, as well as their rent money.

The whole apartment resembled a disaster scene, with the bathroom faring the worst. It looked like my son-in-law had been murdered in there. Blood covered the walls, bathtub, everywhere.

After the robbers left, my daughter went to her sister's apartment, called the police and an ambulance. Her husband needed to be taken to the hospital where he had many stitches on his face, as a result from being beaten.

Life just did not seem fair. In fact, it seemed nothing was fair about it, at all.

The men were never caught, although much later, my daughter realized that she recognized one of the men, when she saw him at her workplace. By then, the police told her it was too late to do anything about it. With no physical evidence and after time elapsing, it would only be her word against his.

My daughter and her family moved from that complex immediately after the robbery. One thing still burdened my heart, though. My other daughter still lived in her apartment, across the hall, in that same building. A building I considered unsafe.

Since this all transpired about the time Gordon was due to return from London and since I would then be looking to purchase a home for myself,

I decided to do something a bit out of the ordinary in an effort to help my daughter and her family. We agreed that we would look for new living accommodations for her and her family.

This way, she could move out of the building, without any trouble from her landlord. She wouldn't have to give the required sixty day notice from the last date of the tenancy, because I would take over her apartment, moving into it and giving immediate notice to vacate.

This way, I wouldn't really have to unpack much, but just move again, once I found the home of my dreams.

Well, as you may well have guessed, things didn't go quite as planned.

Gordon kept telling me I should just stay living in his investment property and not move into that apartment. But, being the stubborn person I tend to be, I did not listen.

He helped me move into the apartment, located not far from where he worked. Immediately after moving all my belongings into the apartment and getting it set up so I could work comfortably, life took another strange turn.

First, I must say that I had a very scary thing happen. While lying awake in my bed one night, the apartment front door opened. I pretended to be asleep, but held tightly to the knife I had been sleeping with. Yes, after what had happened to one of my daughters and her family, I prepared for the worst. On that night, I was glad I had the knife with me.

Nothing happened, though. The man left as quietly and quickly as he entered. Who he was, I have no idea. Against the light from the hallway, only a dark shadow of the outline of the person appeared for me to see. He obviously had a key for both my door and my locking chain lock, or else he had great skill at picking locks.

In any case, I knew in my heart I had truly made a mistake moving into this apartment. To this day, I am glad I helped my daughter and her family leave that place.

Gordon, furious with me for moving into this apartment, demanded I return to his vacant rental property, once again. I refused, because I knew I needed to purchase a place to call my own.

Something else happened to me, though. Something that I never dreamed would happen.

I found out I needed abdominal surgery. Without going into great detail, it is enough to say that after my surgery, I awoke to find that not only had a hernia repair been done, but in addition, the surgeon had relined my whole abdominal cavity. Apparently, due to a problem from a previous surgery, the only thing holding my intestines inside me was my skin.

So, this turned out to be major surgery. Much more major than I ever expected to have.

Gordon took care of me.

Not at my apartment, though. Instead, he moved his single bed from his own home, to next door, the house I had just moved out of.

He also brought over his recliner chair and television. These weren't for him to use, but for me.

He insisted I remain there, where I was safe. He slept on a blow-up air mattress, so I could sleep on his single bed.

He sat on a lawn chair, while I reclined comfortably in his recliner chair.

He cooked for me and provided for my every need, including cleaning and tending to my two incisions. He helped me walk. He took me to physician appointments. He made sure I took my medications. And, basically showed me that he loved me, beyond anything I could imagine.

No one had ever shown me this much love. I knew at this time, that I wanted to marry again. Marry Gordon. But, I just couldn't bring myself to do this.

After one medical checkup, on a day when I was first well enough to drive my vehicle, I wanted to go to the apartment to check on things.

Being Friday, Gordon insisted we not go, for he felt I had already overexerted myself. He said we would go over the next day, when he didn't have to work. Then, he left to go work his afternoon shift at GM.

What did I do? You probably guessed that I got into my car and drove over to the apartment. If you thought this, you would be right; I did it. For some reason, I just felt I absolutely had to go check on my apartment.

As I arrived at the complex, I wondered if I had done the right thing.

Slowly, I made my way up the stairs to the second floor landing. I stood by the front door to my apartment and unlocked the main door lock. Then, I began to slowly open the door, knowing I had to use the key for the chain lock, next.

It was shocking to see the chain lock undone already, *not* unlocked by using a key as it should have been , but rather from the inside of the apartment, by sliding it across and through the interior only access. I heard a voice.

The voice, not from inside the apartment, and not in the hallway or on the staircase, but in my head, somehow sounded like how I would imagine God's voice to sound.

The voice sounded adamant when it told me very slowly, *"Do…not…go… in…there!"*

Why I did the next thing I did, I'll never know.

Instead of immediately hightailing it away from there, I took my left hand and reached in to the interior handle of the door, turned the lock so the door would be once again locked, and shut the door.

Then, with my heart racing, I made my way down the staircase and out to my car. My heart beat so strongly and quickly, like I had been running, but I knew I hadn't been running, for I could hardly walk.

My daughter didn't live far from there, so I drove over to see her. Thinking I would find out that she had been over to water my plants or check on things and had left the chain lock undone, I calmed myself, somewhat.

Unfortunately, she did not tell me she had been over to the apartment. Instead, she told me she had *not* been to the apartment and could not possibly have undone the chain.

Together, we returned to the apartment, thinking we would check on things and everything would be okay. I felt overexerted, exhausted, and over-worried, for no reason, or so I thought at the time.

Wrong, again! We noticed my VCR missing. My computer and printer were gone. Yet, my television still remained. My typewriter sat on the kitchen counter, close to where the apartment's back door had been broken into. The door's glass had been smashed.

We called the police, who told me that I must have been walking in on the robbers, the first time I attempted to enter the apartment. The officer explained that this must have been the case, or else everything of any value would have been taken; not just a few things, with more ready to go out the door.

Wow! Double wow! Triple wow! Be still my heart! While I appeared calm, I felt destroyed, once again. Yet, joyful, that my God had protected me, through this trial.

Talk about an ordeal. You should have been there to have heard Gordon when he found out! Oh, dear! To say he was upset with me for going over to the apartment would be an understatement. It was about the closest thing to furious I can ever recall him being.

Gordon made it clear to me that I might have been injured, mugged, raped or killed, had I entered the apartment, the first time. He made it clear that I should never have gone there without him in the first place.

Oh well; part of me was thankful I had gone there the first time alone. I wouldn't have wanted him or anyone else to be hurt, which could easily have happened. After all, by this time, Gordon had been part of my life for at least fifteen years, or so. Even though we hadn't yet married, I could not imagine living my life without him.

Once again, I faced the fact that life is short. We have no control over any-thing in our lives. God is truly the *only* person in control. He had protected me, once again. Why He loved me this much, I couldn't say, other than to say that He did. And, He does, still.

Chapter Nine

Our Marriage

Lynn & Gordon – Wedding & Honeymoon Cruise

After the close call I had with intruders who stole from me, I did a lot of praying.

Gordon once again asked me to marry him, telling me how much he truly loved me and wanted to take care of me, always. He didn't have to tell me he loved me, for I already knew this.

As you have read, I was the problem, not him.

Leftover lack of confidence, caused by issues I've written about from my earlier life made me feel truly unsure about my judgment. I was afraid to make a decision to marry, because I didn't know if I could trust my feelings.

Knowing Gordon loved me made no difference. After all, other men in my life were supposed to have loved me, but in the end, time proved they didn't.

I needed to sort out myself and my feelings, as well as about what the Bible taught, so I went to my pastor. Actually, I spoke with *our* pastor. By this time, I worshipped at the nearby Baptist church where Gordon had begun worshipping, just before he left for London. Our pastor and I had many conversations together.

In an effort to sort out some feelings about past family troubles, I attended Christian counseling. Eventually, I reached the point where I could commit.

I didn't take this decision lightly. Between my past that haunted me, fear of the future, and potential step-parent problems, I felt terrified.

Besides, how could I trust my own judgment? Hadn't I made numerous mistakes in my life? I truly lacked confidence.

My pastor reminded me that I need to trust God for the outcome concerning any decision I made in my life.

In my heart, I truly wanted to marry Gordon and hadn't yet done so. I *was sinning*, not just by being afraid, but also by not trusting God for the result of any decision I made. So, I prayed more and more about this.

Then, one day life changed. It was not a special day of any sort. We were just together for a while and Gordon asked me once again to marry him.

Later, I found out that friends of his from Amherstburg knew Gordon planned to propose to me, once again. Some of his family also knew his plan. I believe I was the last person to know!

Gordon got down on one knee and proposed marriage to me.

Unlike many times in the past, I didn't say no, this time. Nor, did I say I'd have to think about it. Instead, I confidently said, *yes*! I don't believe either of us could have been happier!

Scheduling our wedding wasn't of huge concern to me, but Gordon insisted we set a date as soon as possible. I think it may have been because he thought I would change my mind!

We looked forward to enjoying a honeymoon together. Neither of us had experienced a honeymoon, even though we had both been married previously.

Trying to think logically, we checked out some travel agents and decided on one, who suggested a Caribbean cruise. Nice! We had each sailed in the past, so we were open to the idea.

We found a holiday we liked and decided to book it as our honeymoon. Our pastor confirmed his and our church's availability and agreed to marry us March 29, the Saturday of Easter weekend.

Believe it or not, that's how we arranged our upcoming union. We set our wedding date based upon our honeymoon plans.

We had relatives stand up with us, as maid of honor and best man. Both our moms were in attendance, as were some other family and friends.

What a perfect day!

My maid of honor insisted I needed arrive at the church *late*. After all, it is rather traditional here in Canada for brides to do this. Although I did not follow this suggestion, our wedding ceremony began later than I ever thought it would.

Even though all preparations were in order, we didn't begin on schedule, for my bouquet had mistakenly been brought into the sanctuary and I didn't want to enter to get it. So, I had to wait until someone finally brought it to me.

Once the processional music began, I proceeded to walk through the sanctuary. I stopped in the aisle, next to where family was seated. Leaning over, I kissed my children and grandchildren in attendance. Upon making my way to join my future husband waiting with our pastor, I could see Gordon grinning from ear to ear, with his eyes emitting happiness I had never seen before. I'll never forget his expression.

Before I say anything more, I must say that at the time of the day of our marriage, I unfortunately was battling an upper respiratory infection.

During our rehearsal, our Pastor had told us to respond as he questioned, meaning that if he asked *will you*, we should reply, *I will*. If he were to say *shall you*, we should respond, *I shall*. And, if he were to say *do you*, our response should be, *I do*.

At the time, I recall asking him which he would say. Our pastor responded that he didn't really know which way he would question us, so we should listen.

Well, being nervous and sickly, I screwed up!

When it came time to ask us the question and say our vows, between headache pain, and not being able to neither breathe nor hear very well, due to the lingering upper respiratory infection, I didn't hear the question.

Even now, I cannot tell you what our pastor asked me. Did he ask *Will you? Shall you?* or *Do you?* I didn't know!

I tried to motion to our pastor that I didn't hear him, but he didn't catch on. Knowing we were being filmed and audio recorded, I didn't want to make a mess of things and ask him to repeat the question! After all, how would that look for posterity!

I expected Gordon to give me a hint, for I thought he understood my problem. I thought he recognized I hadn't heard the question. Instead, Gordon became tense. His eyes grew like saucers. Silently, I chuckled to myself, once I realized he thought I might have been changing my mind, expecting me to turn and run. I didn't really know what to do about this dilemma.

Eventually, I did the only thing I could think of, when my pastor began to look at me with the same puzzled look. I replied, "*I will, shall, do!*"

To my surprise, no one laughed. Although, to this day, every time I think of this, I laugh!

We had a lovely luncheon reception at a nearby hotel restaurant where we, along with our friends and family, celebrated our marriage. The Phantom and Christine serenaded us. What a beautiful memory! One, I'll always remember, with love. Since God was for us, who could be against us?

Chapter Ten

Our Honeymoon

Easter Sunday, the morning after our wedding night, we worshipped at church, enjoyed lunch with family, and set off on our honeymoon.

Gordon's best man and his wife drove us to the Detroit Airport, where we boarded a plane and flew to Miami, Florida.

Knowing that the ten day, deep southern Caribbean cruise didn't leave for a few days yet, we had pre-arranged to pick up a rental car and drive to Key West for a couple of days.

We did this. This was a problem, because we hadn't planned on me being sick like this. And, sick, I was!

Still, our priority was to enjoy our honeymoon. That's why we didn't cancel everything. Instead, I took medications to keep my sinus passages open while flying.

Poor Gordon ended up driving to the southern tip of mainland Florida while I reclined my seat and slept. We stayed overnight, along the way.

Next day, Gordon did all the driving through the Keys until we reached our destination. Key West.

We had a beautiful room, overlooking the Gulf of Mexico.

I tried to make an effort to enjoy some time with Gordon, so we went into the most southern part of the island and looked around. We also went into the hot tub and pool together.

That turned out to be the only time we enjoyed together at that hotel in Key West. Unfortunately, I became so sick, that I could hardly lift my head from the pillow. So, for the duration of our stay there, he spent time alone, taking care of me.

As planned, we left the Keys and drove back to Miami. Once again, Gordon drove, while I rested.

We checked in at our hotel, where we were to stay for the night before we embarked on our cruise. We shopped for medications for me. I thought we should have bought stock in *Walgreen's*, for I felt like we had bought out the store!

Feeling somewhat improved after all that rest, we decided to visit the Miami Zoo. We had a wonderful time there together, even if I felt totally spent by the time we headed back to the hotel.

The next morning, we made our way to the quayside and located the ship. We gave the cruise line representatives our luggage and our passports upon checking in at the counter.

Then we took a seat, for what seemed to be an eternity. We waited and waited. This was not normal. Being patient more than a couple hours past what we thought we'd wait, we were finally asked to line up in order to embark. Finally! Our honeymoon cruise began!

You must have a visual picture in your mind of well over a thousand people lined up, waiting to board the ship, all with eager anticipation.

Then, the announcement came. The cruise lines announced that unfortunately, due to over three hundred people coming off the ship sick, it had been shut down and the cruise, cancelled.

Feeling rather shocked, I waited a few seconds for the announcer to continue and say *only kidding*, being a joke. But, to our dismay, this didn't happen. The cruise truly had been cancelled.

Oh no!

I recall looking at Gordon, also in a state of shock and commenting that this couldn't be happening to us. This *was* to be the only honeymoon we would ever have!

Well, it did happen. The announcer told everyone to go into the claim area to retrieve their luggage, before making our way to the sidewalk outside, where buses would be waiting to take us to nearby hotels.

We experienced an absolute nightmare, that day. People everywhere were shoving others and yelling, angry about what happened. We tried to stay calm, but we were very upset.

Upon arriving at the hotel, we were ushered into a ballroom that held several hundred people. A calypso band played in one corner of the room. Lunch awaited us, on tables filled with sandwiches and salads, plus mouth-watering desserts that we might normally have enjoyed aboard the ship, had we been there.

We were directed by the cruise company representatives to call our travel agents, to change our air flight tickets to fly back to Detroit as soon as possible. The company said they would cover the cost of our flights. Well, with so many people and so few pay phones available in the hotel's hallway, it took several hours before we even had a chance to use a telephone.

In the meanwhile, there were several couples and families who wanted to stay as well as honeymooners like us who didn't want to fly home. We requested the cruise line provide another cruise for us, they insisted they were completely sold out. We didn't believe them.

After finally reaching our travel agent near the close of day, we found out that the cost would be over nine hundred US dollars each, for us to fly back to Detroit, because our existing tickets were non-changeable and new, last minute one-way airfare would have to be purchased.

The cruise line decided, upon learning the excessive cost of our return flight that they would not pay for the tickets after all. Good. We didn't want to go, either.

When they realized they couldn't get rid of about fifty or so of us, they called in a travel agent, who gave us an opportunity to purchase another cruise. No, they wouldn't exchange our existing tickets; we had to purchase another holiday. The cruise line from our cancelled honeymoon would eventually refund us the cost of the cancelled holiday, but not at the time we needed to arrange a replacement. I recall thinking it was good that we had a credit card available to us, to use to make this purchase; otherwise we may not have been able to arrange a honeymoon trip for us, at all!

This holiday didn't travel to the deep southern Caribbean. Instead, the Panama Canal was the main feature. And it didn't leave until the following day, so our whole group needed a place to stay for the night.

Even so, we all purchased tickets on the Panama Canal cruise.

The cruise line whose ship we never sailed on that day, agreed to put us all up in the hotel where we were at the time. They provided us dinner, also.

We were told we could not leave the hotel. Why? They had lost our passports, and would return them to us, in person, when they were located. So, we had to remain available, at the hotel.

Did you get the drift of what I just said?

The cruise line *lost* our passports. While most people had theirs returned to them later that evening, Gordon and I waited until the next morning, about an hour before we were due to be transported to Fort Lauderdale to fly to Jamaica, where we would embark on the Panama Canal cruise.

Believe me when I say we prayed. And, when we received our passports in our hands, we praised God and thanked Jesus!

Had the cruise line not been able to hand us our passports that we needed before we could fly out from the US, we would have had to cancel our second choice honeymoon. But, praise God! He came through for us!

Thank You, Lord! We all were able to board the bus that delivered us to Fort Lauderdale airport.

In hand, we had all the info the cruise line had promised us, along with directions from them on what to do upon returning from our honeymoon cruise. The replacement cruise, being a seven night cruise and not a ten night cruise as the original one had been, meant we again required a place to stay, upon returning to the US. We would be the *only* people who required this, because everyone else was able to arrange transportation home, for themselves.

We were delighted to be guaranteed that when we returned, the cruise line would be putting us up at a nearby hotel in Miami for the extra days, including our meals.

It seemed God *was* in control, after all. Even if our honeymoon didn't happen as we had originally planned.

Flying once more made me nervous, because I had not yet recovered from the respiratory infection. We prayed about it and I seemed to fare well, flying to Montego Bay, Jamaica.

From there, we embarked our awaiting cruise ship! No surprises, here, praise God! Off we went, joyfully, to find our cabin, unpack a bit, and attend the mandatory on-deck emergency lifeboat evacuation drill.

Being sick and feeling at times that I was in a truly living hell I wanted to just relax and heal.

Well, even though we truly were not living in hell, we did visit Hell, on Grand Cayman Island. So, I guess you could say we went to Hell and back, again!

We also visited Key West. With my head somewhat less aching and clearer than it had been at the beginning of our honeymoon, we actually did some sightseeing together; more than the last time we were there.

Together, we stood and had our photo taken at the southernmost tip of the Florida Keys.

We enjoyed Venezuela.

In Colombia, we did some sightseeing, bought coffee (of course!) and even met Juan Valdez! Yes, he was selling the coffee we purchased!

In a dugout canoe, we toured and visited some of the San Blas Islands. On their main island, the chief invited Gordon into his personal tent. Since their tribe is rather short, their chief was drawn to tall men and only gave an invitation to those he thought were special in some way. With Gordon being close to six foot two inches tall and being easy to look at, he made quite an impression on the tribal leader, who invited us to come back to visit!

We cruised in and out of the Panama Canal. By this time, my sick and aching body just wanted to relax, so this proved to be just what the doctor ordered!

After sightseeing in Puerto Limon, Costa Rica, we shopped 'til we dropped. Well, at least I did! How could I resist? The leather goods were just wonderful!

All in all, we had a wonderful time, both with our friends from the cancelled cruise disaster and with others we met aboard our honeymoon ship. Even being sick and pushing myself to do things and not just lie in bed, I must admit I enjoyed this wonderful cruise.

We disembarked at Montego Bay, Jamaica, at the end of the cruise. At the airport, we boarded the plane. A strange fellow that Gordon and I suspected as a drug user, jumped from seat to seat, eventually sitting beside me. Gordon's seat was beside the window, as usual.

This fellow seemed like he had ants in his pants, for he couldn't sit still. We were delayed. The longer we sat on the plane awaiting take-off, the more jumpy this fellow became. When he again changed seats, we were happy!

Then, we found out what caused the delay. Apparently, someone had checked some luggage, but they had not boarded the airplane for the flight.

Consequently, we were delayed until all luggage could be unloaded, the disowned luggage found, removed and the remaining luggage reloaded.

Eventually, our flight took off! I praised God that my ear drums hadn't burst, for they were hurting terribly. This time, we weren't on a direct flight to Fort Lauderdale. We had to fly to Kingston, Jamaica, first, to pick up more passengers.

Upon landing, we blew a tire. Wow! It was a hard landing, to be sure! Many people were afraid, especially since the runway is short, there. As for me, well with being sick, I just felt like dying, anyway!

With this delay, we finally arrived in Fort Lauderdale many hours later than originally scheduled.

When the plane's door opened, officials accompanied by drug-sniffing dogs grabbed the fellow who had been so jumpy, along with a few other people on whose persons were found traces of drugs. Wow! Never before had either of us experienced being held up in this manner!

As directed by the cancelled cruise representative, we took a taxi from the airport to the Miami hotel where we had been told a room would await us.

Upon arriving at the hotel, the desk clerk assured us no reservation was in their records, allowing us to check in.

By this time, after nine p.m., and being literally sick and tired, I produced the information supplied to us, as well as the business card of the cruise line representative who had directed us. The clerk photocopied the card and information and returned them to me, claiming they would try to reach the man.

After a few minutes, they told us we would have to leave, because they could not reach the fellow, claiming they were booked solid for the night. We made it clear we were going nowhere and sat in their lobby.

Again, the desk clerk and manager came to us, telling us we would have to leave. This time, we calmly told them that we were not going anywhere except to the media if they forced us out.

After a couple of more discussions on the subject, they finally found us a room. Even though room service had finished for the night, they sent food up to the room, for us.

After a shower and changing into our comfy nightwear, a tuxedo-clad waiter brought into our suite a lovely table beautifully set for the two of us, complete with a floral centerpiece. Of course, we enjoyed the food, savoring each delicious bite.

Unfortunately, we weren't able to sleep in, the following morning. Our phone rang, early. The front desk clerk had a message for us.

The cruise line representative apparently could not be reached and the cruise line claimed they had no idea we were to be there. Not caring that we had this in writing, they demanded we pack up and vacate the suite.

We did.

In the lobby, we were told once again to leave the premises. By this time, running out of medication and having fever, I could hardly think straight and insisted we were going nowhere.

Eventually, they threatened to call the police. We welcomed this! We also made it clear that if they did not follow through with what their sister corporation had arranged for us and called the police, we would call a lawyer.

We made it clear that we believed they would have wonderful media coverage from every newspaper, radio and television station in Miami.

Imagine how the media would run with a story of us not just being wronged twice, but how they managed to do their best to ruin the *only* honeymoon we would have. Not to mention me being ill, too.

After this last confrontation, we remained in their lobby, with me trying to breathe and my head feeling as if it would blow up. Gordon did his best to make me feel comfortable and reassured me everything would be all right.

He wanted to just leave and find our own way. Being the person I am, I refused to do this. After all, we weren't asking them to do anything that hadn't already been offered us. We were only standing our ground, demanding they follow through on their promise.

When they realized we truly were not going to leave, a desk clerk approached us, explaining there had been a mix up. They claimed an error had been made and that we had been expected at another sister hotel, at the other end of the block, where a reservation awaited us.

They provided a limo to take us to their sister hotel. It turned out to be the same establishment the cruise line had utilized when our original cruise had been cancelled.

The desk clerk there, shocked to see us, claimed that was the quickest reservation she had ever seen filled! Apparently, it had only been made minutes earlier.

Oh well! At least we had a room to relax in, where we could chill out and I could try to recover from my upper respiratory infection. And, at best, the cruise line was fulfilling their promise to us.

After checking in, we once again visited the Walgreen's that we had shopped at previously.

We were comfy in our room and had a gorgeous view.

By the time the day came for us to fly to Detroit and head back to Windsor, we were more than ready to go. You might be wondering why I would write about this. Well, not only did we have a strange honeymoon experience, but I believe that God revealed to us a secret.

The stressful beginning of our marriage would be exactly that, just the *start* of what the future would hold in store for us. While we hoped for our beginning to be an era of our lives where God would bless us with peace and love, things did not work out as planned.

Even though Gordon didn't like the fact that I was ill when we married and spent our whole honeymoon ill, he proved himself to be very patient, loving, and caring. I knew in my heart he truly loved me. And, I loved him.

We looked forward to spending the rest of our lives, together. And we were happy.

There were three people in our marriage: Gordon, me, and God. And even after the somewhat stressful beginning to our married life, we planned to live happily ever after.

Chapter Eleven

Our Married Life

As we settled into married life, Gordon and I made some decisions. First, he moved into the home next door, the one I had lived in, after returning to Windsor.

This made the move fairly simple, because I already had my furniture in place and by adding in his few pieces and personal belongings it proved to be not a difficult task.

Life just seemed to fall into place.

Nothing terrible happened. We began to believe we were being blessed by God, as we walked through life as a married couple.

Our relationship flourished as it never had in the past. Happiness seemed to radiate from both of us.

Even at this time, Gordon didn't really like me selling real estate. He would accompany me on most of my open houses.

I truly loved that about him. He always wanted to not just love me, but protect me as well.

Gordon knew how years earlier, before I worked selling real estate, God had protected me when I had been chased through the courtyard adjacent to the vacant condo I had purchased. Eventually, police caught the fellow and found there had been an outstanding warrant for his arrest, from out in Western Canada.

He also knew that on another occasion, as I worked in real estate showing houses to a couple looking to purchase investment property, I found a vagrant sleeping in a home that should have been empty.

Both times, God had protected me. Even so, Gordon didn't like me entering vacant properties.

Thankfully, I was not hurt in either of these experiences, but Gordon wanted to ensure I would be safe and unharmed. So, on one occasion, when I was scheduled to pre-inspect properties for a client who wanted a waterfront residence, he decided to join me.

As we entered this particular cottage on Riverside Dr. E., just east of the beach area his attitude made an about turn. Prior to entering the structure, he had been rather upset, but as we walked through, Gordon's demeanor changed, totally.

He fell in love with the place and told me he wanted us to purchase it. My heart took a tumble, because I truly didn't think we were right for this home.

By the time we left that property, Gordon had already asked me to prepare an offer. Not once, but several times.

Trying to be diplomatic about the whole situation, I suggested we think about it, pray about it, and ask God to give us wisdom and direction. I also let him know my personal and professional opinion regarding the property.

I truly didn't like the idea of buying it. Oh, the cottage seemed perfectly sized and comfortable for our needs, being about fifteen hundred square feet. However, it needed some work in order to make it suitable for us and I didn't want to be living in another property that needed work.

Suggesting we ask God seemed to quiet Gordon's pleading requests, at least for the evening. He agreed. We prayed about it.

By the next day, he spoke about it, again.

We had already planned a flight to Las Vegas and a car trip throughout the Southwestern US, so I suggested we delay a decision on the house. He agreed, because he understood that I needed time to do the extra work of writing an offer; time that I really couldn't spare.

As happens whenever it seems I am preparing to leave on holiday, I became busier than I had time for with my real estate work. Then, adding to my stress, Gordon changed his mind. He wanted me to write an offer on the property.

He told me that if I didn't find time to write an offer, he'd call another realtor. Ha! Sure!

Once again, I managed to coax him into waiting until we returned from our holiday, assuring him that if God planned this home for us, it would still be there waiting, after we returned from our trip. He seemed to be more relaxed after this discussion.

Now, I don't want you to get a wrong impression, here. My efforts were not an attempt to try to be the leader in our relationship.

Being Christian and having read God's word, the Bible, and attending Bible study for many years, I realized that ultimately, as my husband, Gordon held the position of being the head of our household. The ultimate authority with regards to decision making on our behalf didn't belong to me, but rather, to him.

However, as a realtor and his wife, I felt I had to state my case, encouraging him to listen and understand my opinion, regarding this property he so badly wanted.

Did Gordon listen? Yes. Did he agree? No. He wanted that house, and nothing more could be said about it!

Still, realizing work truly rushed me off my feet, he relented. As it turned out, work kept me busy right up to a few hours before our scheduled flight's take off time.

We enjoyed ourselves on our trip to the Southwestern US. We travelled from Las Vegas, to other cities like Los Angeles, San Diego, and of course, Lake Havasu City, Arizona, where we were due to visit with a cousin of mine, who lived there.

During the time we were away on holiday, Gordon never stopped talking about that property.

Arriving back in Windsor, work kept me just as busy as I had been before we flew out on holiday. Gordon patiently waited for me to write the offer. I kept hoping he would change his mind, but he didn't.

About two weeks after returning, I just could not put it off any longer. I wrote the offer. Either that had to happen or Gordon, as he had promised me, would truly call another realtor.

Needless to say, after some negotiation, the offer became an agreement, and we soon moved into our new-to-us matrimonial home. Then he sold the house next door to where we resided upon first becoming married.

Gordon decided he didn't want to sell the other house, yet; the one we had been living in. One of my daughters and her family lived there for many years.

We hired a contractor friend to do work at our new bungalow. We made some alterations, like adding shelving in the storage room and replacing the roof of this cottage-style bungalow.

We had the living and dining rooms leveled off, so that the whole area became one giant room without any step down to a sunken area. We also replaced a window in this now great room with a patio door, so we would have a more unrestricted view of our yard and the waterfront.

Renovations took somewhat longer than we originally anticipated. Not that I could blame the workers, because it seemed everyone felt like they did, when they stood or sat in our great room. Everyone seemed to just want to relax and hang out. I cannot tell you how many times I entered our cottage, to find workers sitting, relaxing, and enjoying the view!

Relaxation seemed to affect all who took the time to look outside, even our carpenter workers. A calm feeling just seemed to come over all who experienced spending time, looking out onto the water. Thank God they were paid by the job and not by the hour!

I must admit, after we moved in, we were comfy there. Gordon felt like we had won the lottery! A dream of his had been fulfilled, living on the waterfront!

Being a narrow, but very long lot, Gordon sure was a trooper when it came to cutting the lawn, for I could not have physically done this. He also took pride in keeping the doors and windows on the water side, clean. My jobs, being a wife, pertained to the rest of the inside of our home, of course.

To give you an idea of what we experienced daily, looking out from our great room to the left we would see the Detroit River; to the right, Lake St. Clair. Directly forward, across from us, the US. The varied shades of green and blue began at the edge of our home and made their way not just to the water, but up through the sky into the heavens.

Gentle wave action filled our heads with memories of being on the seas, cruising to destinations in foreign lands.

Ships passing both night and day, along with sailboats silently drifting from lake to river created a landscape of ever-changing variety.

We listened to birds chirping daily, as they hid in a nearby bush. As a wedding gift, we had been given a unique bird feeder stand. It was a rather tall structure, being made from one steel rod that stood well over eight feet high. On the bottom were prongs that allowed us to firmly set it into the ground. The top held a painted, wooden design of a bird house, being flat, not constructed three dimensionally. However, there was a perch that stuck out from the painted on entrance to the birdhouse, where birds actually landed to rest. Just below the faux birdhouse was a cross-arm, which allowed us to hang two feeders. Gordon installed it where we would be able to look out and watch as eager mouths filled hungry tummies.

We kept track of the kinds of birds we found on the water side of our property. In total, we found over forty varieties, ranging from blue jays, to cardinals, to hummingbirds, to Canada Geese.

In fact, one winter, we cared for and fed an injured bird, whose wing appeared to be broken. This Canada goose, we named Goosie; while we didn't know for sure, we presumed she was female. At first, she was fearful of us and wouldn't allow us to touch her, even in an effort to provide treatment for her. Eventually, realizing we meant her no harm, she would waddle up to us, to take food from us.

By the time spring arrived, Goosie was happy to see us, when we opened our door. She made many attempts to enter our home, but this was something we wouldn't allow. We didn't think our two elderly, baby-boy-pussycats would be too happy, if she joined them!

We sometimes felt badly for her, especially when she would approach us at our sliding patio door. She made attempt after attempt to gain entry there. Each time, she would hit her beak, as she tried to peer inside at us.

Eventually, being healed, Goosie left us and flew away with a flock headed north for the summer season. Gordon was sad; so was I. We missed her, but were grateful God had brought this wonderful gift into our lives, even if not permanently.

With or without distractions of various kinds from boaters, swimmers, and water sports enthusiasts, we enjoyed the calm, relaxing feeling when we just sat there and looked outside. It filled us with a peace that we believed could only come from God.

That is, until we had flooding occur. The Windsor Star had a photo on the front page, showing a woman's car engulfed by water at a level that prevented her from driving her vehicle. Her car was directly in front of our house, which was also prominently displayed showing water surrounding it! The article claimed it was the worst in over twenty-five years!

I must admit, I personally had never seen flooding like this.

As it happened, I had been working at home, as usual. As a realtor, most of my job can be done from there.

In the afternoon, I took a break to curl up in my comfy chair. As I spoke on the telephone, looking out at the lake, something happened that I never thought I would ever see.

I can recall gasping aloud. The lake seemed to lift up at the far side. Visually, it reminded me of a kiddy pool, the kind with three or so inflated rings. In order to empty these pools, one must lift up one side, causing the water to overflow on the other.

Well, this is exactly what it looked like from where I sat. The lake lifted up on the far side and the water came rolling in, like a mini tsunami.

In fact, before I could finish my sentence to the caller, the water rose up my patio door. By the time it reached more than a foot or so, in this short time frame, I sat speechless.

Lights began to flicker. Instead of a basement, we had a crawl space, where our duct work, wiring and structural support, was located. The water flooding into the crawl space must have soaked our wiring. I quickly turned off the lights to avoid an even greater disaster.

Gordon arrived from work shortly thereafter, finding about two feet of water surrounding our home. Fortunately, he managed to park in a less water-logged area, nearby. While it was discouraging, he was not shocked about seeing the water. Before punching out at the factory, a work mate who had also heard about the disaster that hit our area told him about it and suggested we needed all the help we could muster. Gordon's friend loaned us another pump.

With three pumps working hard to remove water from our home, we were able to keep the water level somewhat under control, flooding only our ground level storage room and of course the crawl space. After setting up the third pump, Gordon and I decided to leave. Due to the darkness of the sky and the storm worsening, our lights that were once again turned on began to flicker.

We rounded up our two baby-boy-pussycats, placing them into their carrying cases. At nearly twenty years of age, they didn't want to leave. Of course, neither did we, but we knew we weren't safe there, with wet wiring.

While I packed us some clothing, Gordon removed heartfelt keepsakes, like family photos. Then we made our way to his mom's, where we stayed for about two weeks.

We were grateful to be comfortable staying there while being temporarily displaced. This not only gave us time to clear our heads, it also gave us time and the ability to be able to deal with our insurer.

Well, in the end, there was no insurance to worry about. Initially, the company called in a restoration specialist to lift our carpeting and use commercial dryers to dry out our home.

However, once insurance company found out the newspaper had written about it being the worst flooding in more than twenty-five years, and since the whole area flooded, they determined that this to be an act of God and refused to cover us for any structural damage that happened.

We praised God that there hadn't been more done than what we had to deal with. After all, if it had been much worse, we wouldn't have been able to continue living there. We fixed what we could and made the decision to not proceed with further major structural repairs, because we knew that no matter much we enjoyed living there, our cottage had become virtually a tear-down. As a result of the flood, it now needed to be rebuilt.

We knew we were not going to even consider rebuilding, given the fact that Gordon was thinking about accepting an early-retirement package from work. We knew once he retired, we would be moving into different living accommodation, because we wanted freedom that could only be obtained by living somewhere where we could lock the door and take off to destinations of our dreams.

In our area, on the waterfront, many properties were like ours; cottage-style homes. However, people were purchasing with the intent of tearing them down, and rebuilding mega-homes. More and more of these new mini-mansions were being built, all the time.

We decided that to be financially prudent, we wouldn't spend a small fortune to rebuild, especially knowing we had actually experienced people knocking on our door privately, to purchase our property for such a purpose.

Once we were cleared to do so, we returned home and lived comfortably once again.

We were grateful to God for protecting us, even through this disaster. Some of our neighbors found themselves in worse shape than us. Many lost furniture and keepsakes that could not be replaced.

So, we felt blessed and praised God. We had each other. We had our home. We had our furry family. And, we were happy.

Chapter Twelve

Changes

Even though we were happy together at the beginning of our marriage, life began to become stressful.

At first, I thought I imagined the fact that Gordon appeared to be changing. He seemed to be moody at times, with no provocation.

I recall asking him repeatedly if I had done something to upset him. He always replied that he wasn't unhappy with me, for any reason.

As this trend continued, Gordon began telling me he didn't feel the greatest. He began to experience physical ailments and conditions that he hadn't had before.

In addition, he developed an intermittent hand tremor that could go from being non-existent, to being so bad he had to grasp his right hand with his left, in an effort to stop his hand from shaking out of control.

We visited our family doctor.

After doing blood work, our physician told us he didn't believe there was anything to worry about. He told us he believed Gordon didn't have cancer. Of course, he had never been present when he experienced the tremor or any other of the major changes we noted. At first, we thought of this like when people go to the dentist. After all, how many times have we had pain, yet when the time comes to finally sit in the dentist's chair, our pain disappears! If you haven't experienced phenomena like this, I applaud you, because I believe most of us have.

In any case, after receiving an all clear from our physician, Gordon refused to go back to see him, at least for a while.

Eventually, I insisted Gordon return to the doctor. I went with him and assured him that my husband's symptoms were real and getting worse, not better.

We also explained that Gordon seemed to be having times of extremely moodiness. Not consistently, but intermittently; it seemed to be triggered by something that upset him.

In addition, when a stressful incident happened to Gordon, instead of remaining calm, as he always had in the past, he would fly off the handle.

This problem became so much a part of normal life that I found myself feeling like a police officer or a counselor, trying to take control of situations so Gordon would be removed from the stress.

Back to the doctor we went.

Our physician decided that maybe Gordon suffered from stress and prescribed medication to help him relax. To my surprise, it didn't work.

Instead, I found him even more fragile, emotionally. He would lose his temper over virtually nothing at all. And, when this happened, it seemed like he couldn't get control of it, again.

I had seen this in him when years earlier Gordon found he couldn't deal with losing the old me in the bus collision and had developed a drinking problem. He would become enraged and sometimes get out of control.

It upset him terribly when I asked him if he had begun drinking, again.

This may sound insensitive, but I believed it absolutely necessary to ask, because when he had his earlier problem, he didn't sit around drinking, or go out with friends to a bar. Instead, he hid it around anywhere he could, so others did not know what he was up to.

Gordon assured me he had *not* once again begun drinking.

In the past, this problem had been part of the reason our relationship had been an on-again-off-again one. It contributed to me many times saying no, when he proposed marriage to me, even after he had given up drinking.

I wondered if I had indeed made a mistake marrying him. I wondered if I could trust him, at first.

I prayed about this situation. Of course, for healing for Gordon, but also about whether I felt distrustful because of his past problem or due to the current situation.

With the subject coming up repeatedly, I realized that I could not see any indicators of his drinking, other than his symptoms.

In addition to the previous symptoms, he began experiencing others, like not being able to think straight, at times. The signs of his illness continued to be intermittent.

Back to the doctor we went, where he was prescribed a different medication to help him relax.

No matter how much we tried to impress upon him the severity of this situation, nothing much changed.

I became very frustrated with the whole situation.

Life grew more stressful when Gordon's mood swings worsened. On several occasions, they even involved other people.

In one instance, while he had every right to be upset with our neighbor next door, things got out of hand. The police were eventually involved. Not good.

No matter how much we prayed about his situation, it seemed that God didn't answer in a way that would provide the healing he needed.

Gordon assured me that he had not been doing anything addictive in nature to incite or encourage this type of behavior. He assured me that since he rededicated his life to Jesus, he would never again drink.

Then, I noticed something different with his moods.

When he stopped taking the medication that our doctor had prescribed, the severity of his anger decreased. However, something else seemed to change.

More and more, Gordon spent time in bed, not feeling well. Our doctor told him he had irritable bowel syndrome. His list of ailments grew.

Then I began to notice a bit of a pattern. He would become enraged over something; it didn't have to be major, for any stress would set him off.

When he became so enraged that even he could not stand being around himself he would head to bed, to lie down. This made me happy at times, for this provided the only form of relief we found.

Gordon had always been a hard worker, dedicated to his employment and to the idea of providing for his family, so he rarely missed work, even when truly ill. When an episode climaxed, after a few hours of rest he relaxed and the anger waned. He would be very sorry for flying off the handle and usually asked me to forgive him. I always did.

In my heart, I knew there was something wrong.

As his condition grew worse, when he awoke after a mood swing episode, he felt not only remorseful, but physically ill in a different way, exhibiting a completely different result.

The diarrhea that occurred as he came out of the anger phase caused him much distress, even causing him to stop on his way to work, sometimes several times, to find a washroom to use. I can recall him laughing and telling me he was thankful for the many Tim Horton's coffee shop locations that provided refuge for his symptoms. He bravely tried to make light of it, but we both knew it wasn't really funny.

This cycle he experienced of stress, followed by anger, rage, feeling physically ill, having to lie down, getting up feeling ill in a different manner, followed by diarrhea and other physical ailments, continued to worsen.

I cannot even recall how many times we returned to our physician, for medical help. Eventually, we together requested he see a psychiatrist, thinking this might be an emotional problem.

Gordon suffered, and I suffered, too. Not just being upset for my husband's physical conditions that seemed to be worsening, but also due to having to deal with all the fallout that occurred with others, that the bouts of anger brought about. I found myself extremely stressed. Even so, I relied on God to help me through this ordeal.

I loved my husband.

We waited to hear back, regarding the referral to a psychiatrist. Month after month, OHIP paid for Gordon to see our family physician, either alone or with me, only to be told that he had no response, yet.

This went on for about three years. All this time, experiencing trauma worsening to the point where he prayed God would take him home to heaven, to be with Him.

Once again, I wondered if my husband experienced deep depression. I couldn't speak with our physician about this with him present, so I went to see him, alone. I made it clear I visited my doctor to speak to him as an advocate.

During our conversation, I tried to impress upon him the need for Gordon to see a psychiatrist.

I explained his mood swing pattern once again and assured him that the intensity and frequency had increased to the point where even I felt physically at risk. He instructed me to leave or call the police if I felt threatened.

Yes. You read correctly.

Our family physician didn't seem concerned for Gordon at all. He simply and calmly told to leave my husband or call the police, if he became a physical threat to me.

How would this help him?

I told him I had no intention of leaving Gordon. I also told him that being Christian, God didn't give permission for me to leave my husband over a health issue, even one as severe as this one. I reminded him that I had taken a vow for better and for worse, for richer and for poorer, 'til death do us part.

I might have considered lashing out at our doctor, but I walked with the Lord and I refrained, for I knew it wouldn't help Gordon's situation.

So, instead, I asked him how he would feel within himself, if Gordon died and further commented that if he was waiting for him to kill himself, he might just get his wish.

Then, it seemed, he took me seriously and within a couple of weeks, Gordon had an appointment with a psychiatrist.

He hadn't known I had gone to our physician to plead on his behalf. I didn't tell him, for a long time afterwards.

Together, we prayed about his need for healing, for relief from his pain, both physical and emotional.

We were certain God would provide healing for Gordon. We counted on it, because we trusted in Him for everything in our lives.

Chapter Thirteen

Leading Up To Diagnosis

We were both so very happy Gordon was finally going to see a psychiatrist, after waiting about three years for an appointment.

Do you think our medical system was overburdened? I did. We did. Even so, we were grateful.

At one of our hospitals, we met with a very nice psychiatrist who spoke first with Gordon then with me.

After hearing from both of us, about the symptoms and pattern Gordon experienced and even speaking with us with regards to my husband's past stresses of life, we heard something we found to be shocking. The doctor told us he didn't think Gordon had an emotional problem.

What? This suggestion was almost too shocking to comprehend, at first.

This psychiatrist let us know that his preliminary suspected diagnosis wouldn't be told to us at that time, because he needed to schedule tests, to obtain further information.

Upon our next meeting with this psychiatrist, we got some results. The test results didn't support his original theory

Still, convinced this *was* a medical problem of some sort, he told us that Gordon needed to have an MRI scan done of his brain.

Since the psychiatrist was due to leave Canada the following week for South Africa, where he worked for half the year, he could not order the MRI. He directed us to have our family physician order it.

Leaving there, we were happy and sad all at the same time. Happy and confident we were in good hands. Sad that we weren't going to have further assistance from this angel of a physician that God had provided us.

We returned to our family physician a few days later, allowing enough time for the psychiatrist's report to be received by him.

We thought we would receive the assistance we needed to get Gordon's required MRI ordered, but we were wrong. Instead of ordering the test, our doctor said he didn't see any need.

We were shocked, even devastated. At first, I didn't think I'd heard correctly. But, unfortunately, I had. Our physician had no intention of involving himself further in this matter.

At the very least, Gordon needed to be able to see another psychiatrist. We hoped this one would be receptive to the idea of ordering an MRI scan for him.

Our physician agreed to make another referral request.

Even so, when we left his office, we were immensely discouraged.

Trying to encourage Gordon, I made light of the situation and suggested we go to see a doctor we knew who worked at a walk-in clinic. He had always been very good with us, whenever we had seen him in the past. We were sure he would order the MRI scan Gordon required, but we were wrong. He wouldn't do it, claiming restrictions on what he could and could not do for those who were not his family practice patients. In his opinion, we needed to have either our family physician or a specialist order the MRI.

Anyone who knows how our wonderful, but broken medical system works here in Ontario is aware that due to the shortage of doctors, not everyone has a physician they can call their family doctor.

To make matters worse, there is such a backlog of people without a doctor that walk-in clinics are over-burdened with needy patients. Our government has also limited what walk-in clinic physicians can do for their patients.

This pinwheel effect began all over again. We visited other physicians at walk-in clinics who had given Gordon good treatment when our family doctor was not available. All to no avail, for they too believed our medical system tied their hands. All referred us back to our family physician. In retrospect, it seems like we would have almost been better off if we had not had a family physician, at all!

Throughout this time period, Gordon became more and more depressed.

He didn't have to tell me, for I could see it. Besides, the pattern of mood-swing/illness progressed. Instead of happening once every few days, it came to occur almost daily. Eventually, I could no longer see when one episode ended and another began.

Month after month we waited for another psychiatrist to be assigned to Gordon's case.

I cannot even recall how long we waited. It seemed like forever.

As time went on, it became harder and harder for Gordon to deal with his situation. He spent much of his time lying in bed, leaving me alone. I began to feel rather depressed as well.

With our healthcare system, we don't have the right to just go outside our country to obtain medical treatment. We need forms signed by physicians who will attest to the need. Then approval by OHIP is required.

People sometimes are misled thinking our medical coverage is free to us. It's not. We pay for it, through taxation. One thing we realized is the fact that no one but physicians had control over our healthcare. We certainly didn't.

Eventually, life became such a burden that a friend of mine took me to a group called *Celebrate Recovery* or CR for short. If you are not familiar with CR, you might want to check it out, especially if you are in the midst of a trial you are finding difficult to bear.

Most people considering a recovery program think of Alcoholic Anonymous or possibly other programs of a similar nature. Certainly CR *is* a program suitable for someone who needs support for a drug or alcohol problem, but it is not limited to this.

CR is a twelve-step, Christ-centered program run by trained volunteers who organize weekly meetings, usually in churches. The group begins with praise and worship, meaning songs and prayer. Then there is usually either a speaker who gives testimony or a lesson taught.

People break up into smaller groups; men with men, and women with women. In the meeting I attended, there were sub-groups for all sorts of needs, like substance abuse, marital problems and divorce, sexual assault, and more.

Everyone had the choice on a meeting by meeting basis which unit they felt they needed to sit in with. If someone didn't know where they should go, or if no cluster was available for their particular need, they usually attended a grouping for *hurts, habits, and hang-ups*.

For this activity, we usually sat in a circle. Everyone had an opportunity to speak and share something about their situation or stress they were feeling or talk about whatever they felt they needed to say. Everything spoken of is held in strict confidence.

All small gatherings opened and closed in prayer.

Afterwards, we once again all congregated for coffee and snacks that people brought to share.

CR had been a wonderful support to me when I needed it. I eventually participated in a year-long Bible study program, set up to assist me in becoming a leader for the group.

However, life at home became even more stressful. Gordon came out to CR on several occasions, but he didn't really feel comfortable participating.

I understood him feeling that any sort of meeting certainly would not do anything to heal him. However, he stopped going, not for that reason, but rather, because someone had betrayed his confidence. CR ended for Gordon — he then refused to attend, with or without me.

When I would go on a Friday evening, I really didn't feel badly about leaving Gordon, alone. Usually, when he wasn't working, he was home in bed. For by this time, he spent almost every evening lying down. His world had shrunk to work and rest.

Even though my heart broke so very badly for Gordon, there were times when I felt already widowed.

Where *was* God? How could this be His plan? Why hadn't He answered our prayers for healing for Gordon? Being such a difficult time, I can hardly even describe it to you.

There came a time when CR support, prayer with my prayer partner, and my prayer time with Gordon no longer helped me through. I went to our pastor; a gentle man, but unwavering in his commitment to the Lord. He always spoke truth, but in love.

He listened to me as I explained everything I've written about concerning Gordon's health problems. He told me about one certain physician who worshipped at our church; head of endocrinology at one of our local hospitals. He offered to introduce me to him the following Sunday and I gratefully accepted. If Gordon was well enough to attend, he would also have the opportunity to meet the doctor.

Sunday morning, we approached our pastor and as we were talking, a sister-in-Christ, a retired physician, overheard us and volunteered to introduce us to this specialist.

Isn't it wonderful how God works?

Our friend introduced us and explained to this specialist that Gordon needed help; to our delight he listened and asked a couple of questions. He directed us to request an ASAP referral to his office from our family physician. Within a few weeks, we had an appointment to see him.

Hope began to arise, once again. I could see an improvement in Gordon's emotional state. I praised God for this.

Together, we praised God for providing an opportunity for help for Gordon. For, without this help, he truly felt lost. Not lost in the sense that he didn't have hope in the Lord, for he always had joy in the Lord, but lost in the sense that he was destined to suffer physically, until he died.

Chapter Fourteen

Diagnosis

A few weeks later, Gordon and I together attended a medical appointment with the specialist who worships at our church. He patiently listened while we explained all that had happened in the past concerning Gordon, his health, and what the psychiatrist who left Canada had told us. We asked him to order the MRI that Gordon needed, but he suggested he do some tests, first.

The doctor ordered Gordon's blood and urine tests. Once the results were obtained, we returned to the specialists' office.

The results from the testing didn't really show any sort of serious problem. Of course, we didn't really know what the doctor searched for, but he didn't find it. Consequently, the specialist refused to order the MRI, claiming he saw no evidence warranting the need for the scan.

Once again, we were disappointed we hadn't found a physician willing to order the MRI that the psychiatrist said Gordon needed.

Unforgettable upset on his face clearly showed his feelings. He pleaded with the specialist to grant our request, to no avail. He still refused.

Our brother-in-Christ stood up and opened the door; he waited for us to exit the examination room. We stood up to leave.

I walked out first. Gordon, behind me, turned and put out his foot, preventing the door to the room from shutting. He made one final request from the specialist. I recall him saying, *"Doctor, please just allow me to have the MRI. I pray you will do this for me. If you do, I will never ask anything of you, again."*

Never before had I ever seen him like this. Usually, if someone didn't want to comply with a request that he made of any kind, he would thank the person, move on, and decide that God's will had been done. But, this *was* different. He knew in his heart he needed the scan.

Much to our surprise, our fellow Christian reopened the door and guided us back into the examination room. He agreed to order the MRI.

Within a couple of weeks, Gordon had his MRI. Much to our surprise, on a Sunday evening he went to the hospital to have his test done.

The following morning while Gordon was at work, our telephone rang. It was early Monday morning when I heard the voice of the specialist.

I don't know about you, what you would do if this happened to you, but it was shocking to me, for *never* before had any physician *ever* phoned me at home! Immediately upon hearing his voice, I knew he'd found something wrong in Gordon's MRI.

He didn't call me Mrs. McKenzie, but spoke to me as a friend, calling me… *Lynn.*

After identifying himself, he didn't speak immediately with regards to Gordon's test results, but chatted for a moment.

Then, he let me know that Gordon had to return to the hospital for more pictures. Something had shown up in the MRI. He had a brain tumor.

Trying to comprehend all this, my mind tried to decide whether to be happy or sad. We had known for a long time that something had to be drastically wrong with him. Getting someone with medical authority to listen to him, or us, had proven to be a difficult task. In my opinion, it could only be compared to pulling teeth, stressful, painful, and almost impossible for an inexperienced person.

Despite our concern for his health and well being, it was gratifying to be reassured that we weren't losing our minds. Hearing from the specialist even, with bad news, reflected in our feeling of relief.

Gordon went back for more pictures, followed by a referral to a neurosurgeon.

When we met with the neurosurgeon, we were happy he had someone looking after him.

Together, we prayed for God's involvement in this whole process. We prayed that God planned some form of treatment, through medications or surgery. We were sure He would provide healing.

We met at the hospital with the neurosurgeon. To our surprise, he showed us the actual MRI and scan results. The neurosurgeon pointed out the exact location of Gordon's brain tumor.

As he talked, I just looked at the picture. It didn't look good. The doctor explained to us that the greater cause of concern was the location, rather than the size of the tumor.

Being in the very centre of the brain, seated on the brain stem meant no chance for Gordon to have traditional surgery to remove it; in addition, no chance for biopsy to check for malignancy, either.

About that time, the neurosurgeon took my arm and asked me if I needed to sit down. After letting the specialist know I did not feel faint, I turned to Gordon. His expression showed nothing. No shock. No disappointment—nothing.

Our discussion regarding treatment wasn't limited to the subject of surgery. The neurosurgeon made it very clear: No treatment of any kind existed for Gordon's tumor. No medicine, no drugs of any kind, nothing to shrink the growth and nothing to kill it existed.

When we left the hospital, you would think we were without hope. Certainly, both Gordon and I were in shock, but we weren't without hope.

How could anyone be without hope, if he had Jesus in his heart!

Chapter Fifteen

Our Response

After receiving the not so great news from the neurosurgeon, we went home. After the shock wore off, I began to panic. Gordon seemed calm. We had planned to drive out west to San Francisco that holiday season. At first, I thought we would cancel this, but Gordon insisted we needed to go.

December that year, with extremely warm temperatures, made our prospect of travelling a unique and truly unusual occurrence. In fact, the weatherman claimed the temperature to be about seventy degrees Fahrenheit in Rapid City, S. Dakota. We packed up and took off to relax on our trip, for we knew nothing could change our situation by staying at home, fretting about Gordon's health.

As we left, on our way to see Mount Rushmore, I began sickening with a sinus problem. By the time we reached Rapid City, I could hardly breathe and felt terribly ill with fever.

We located a church with a Christmas Eve service and one with a Christmas Day service. Then, we checked in at a hotel, had dinner, and settled in to rest.

Awaking the next day, Christmas Eve, I felt even worse. I recall thinking that I shouldn't be the one becoming ill with a respiratory problem, when Gordon needed healing the most! How fair was that?

Of course, fairness had nothing to do with it.

We visited Mount Rushmore and drove through areas where we had deer, antelope, and buffalo all around us. The roads, which would normally be closed due to heavy snow at this time of year, were open due to the fall-like weather. We enjoyed an absolutely beautiful day! Afterwards, we drove around and saw Crazy Horse.

We had a wonderful day, together, finishing with an evening of worship at the Christmas Eve service.

I awoke Christmas Day feeling deathly ill. Consequently, Gordon went to worship at the Christmas Day service alone.

When he arrived back at the hotel, his face gleamed with excitement! During the church service, he noticed there were many Native Americans who arrived late and departed as quickly as they could at the end of the service. Afterwards, he had spoken with the pastor, who explained he reached out to the Native community in Christian love and they had responded. Gordon felt blessed.

We had been hearing about flooding and roads being washed out in areas we would have to drive through on our way to San Francisco. That, along with me being ill, led to Gordon's decision we shouldn't drive any further west. In fact, he thought we should drive home. Boxing day, we packed up and left Rapid City. My fever still raged.

Just before we approached Omaha, Nebraska, I felt better, and told Gordon. He laughed, claiming I just didn't want to drive towards Windsor! I let him know that seriously, all of a sudden my fever broke. I no longer felt ill.

Since we had to either turn off at Omaha to drive to Detroit, or change direction to go somewhere else, Gordon suggested we stay there, to see if I would still be feeling better after a good night's rest. I agreed.

The next morning, I still felt better, with no sign of fever. We talked about where we could go from there. Certainly, we weren't going to head west, again.

Instead, we decided to drive to one of Gordon's favorite places to visit— Treasure Island, Florida. We took off, heading south, with a stop in New Orleans on the way. We enjoyed a short stay there. But, the best was of course the lovely time we shared on Treasure Island.

We made sure that on our way home, we drove through Orlando. Whenever we vacationed on Treasure Island, we usually made our way there, before heading back to Canada. As we did any time we were near that area, we stopped in to worship at a church we had worshipped at many times. As in the past, people recognized us and we were welcomed. We asked for prayer, for healing, for Gordon. We received prayer that day and were grateful for the promise of continued prayer.

God blessed us. He gave us this time together, to be able to come to terms with Gordon's condition in a relaxed environment.

Mostly, we were grateful that He gave us hope.

Chapter Sixteen

Second Opinion

Arriving home, we knew what we needed to do.

We asked friends and family to pray for Gordon's healing. We were convinced God would heal him of this brain tumor.

The neurosurgeon wanted to keep an eye on his condition, so in the beginning, Gordon had regular MRIs. This way, all concerned would know whether or not the tumor grew.

I searched the internet, hoping to find practical help. Then, a friend told me about Gamma Knife radiosurgery. They had heard that this laser-type surgery could be obtained in Michigan.

I researched, quickly! Not only did I become educated regarding the surgery itself, but I learned of an updated version as well: Cyber Knife surgery.

It was disappointing that Cyber Knife was not yet available, but Gamma Knife radiosurgery was being done in three cities in Canada.

Realizing that if Gordon had this type of surgical treatment, the surgeon could blast the tumor, destroying it, we both felt like God had provided the answer to our prayers. We praised God and thanked Jesus!

Gordon's Neurosurgeon did not use the Gamma Knife technique, nor was it available in our city, but he had made himself familiar with it. It shocked us that he, being familiar with the process, hadn't mentioned it to us.

He explained that here in Canada, the *only* people who qualify for this surgical procedure, are confirmed cancer patients. Since Gordon couldn't have a biopsy for the same reason he couldn't have traditional surgery, no one could confirm any malignancy.

He explained to us that Gordon would probably have been made a vegetable, suffered paralysis, brain damage, lost his sight or hearing, or experienced other effects from his brain being physically cut into.

Due to Canada's requirement, the neurosurgeon couldn't even refer him to a Gamma Knife radiosurgery specialist.

The pinwheel had begun, all over again. We didn't lose hope. We prayed and I researched.

Gamma Knife, only done in Canada in three centres, one out west, one in Montreal, and one centre in Toronto, appeared to be of no help to Gordon.

Our brother-in-the-Lord specialist who helped by ordering Gordon's original MRI made a referral to Toronto, at the hospital where Gamma Knife surgery could be done.

Gordon's referral was to a traditional surgeon, like the one in Windsor. But, we were hopeful, praying this newly acquired specialist would be more familiar with the benefits of Gamma Knife radiosurgery, since it was currently being done at his own hospital. We prayed he would make a referral for Gordon, to where he could receive treatment.

We prayed he would sign papers for our medical system to give us permission to take Gordon out of our country to receive either the Gamma Knife radiosurgery or the Cyber Knife surgery, in an effort to provide Gordon a cure. Actually, we were *convinced* he would sign the paperwork.

We prayed about it, because we had found no one in Windsor who would sign the paperwork. Our family physician couldn't; it had to be a specialist. Our brother-in-the-Lord felt he was not the proper type of specialist to be able to have this approved, since he was not a brain surgeon.

Only Gordon's neurosurgeon in Windsor could have done this, but he hadn't. We wondered if it was a case of not wanting to get involved with our medical system, or with the responsibility and paperwork that went along with it. It appeared to us that they have greater responsibility to our government than to their patients. We believe our physicians must be under great pressure to keep patients within our borders. It took us over four hours to drive to the hospital. We patiently waited to see the neurosurgeon.

The doctor entered the room and took a seat. We handed him a copy of Gordon's MRI and a letter from the referring specialist.

He took a few seconds to read the letter and promptly told Gordon that he could do nothing for him. He never asked any questions, nor did he even look at the MRI.

After making that statement, the specialist got up and went to leave the room.

Shocked, I called the doctor's name, asking him to spare us another minute or two, just as he walked through the door.

I asked him if he would please complete the paperwork necessary for our medical system to give Gordon permission to go out of country for the treatment. He replied that he wouldn't.

Wow! Talk about disheartening!

We contacted our friends, who lived in the suburbs and let them know the result of our brief appointment. They were as shocked as we were.

We had hoped to stop on our way back to Windsor to visit some other friends who had moved to the Milton area, but we didn't. Gordon just wanted to go home.

He didn't do much talking as we drove over four hours, once more—he was too upset. Who wouldn't be?

My heart broke for him. Not just because it was upsetting to realize we had once again bumped up against what I call *The Glass Wall*, where we could see treatment, but not access it, but mainly because I could sense a difference in him.

Instead of being confident that God would provide, he told me that we had to face the fact that he wouldn't receive any help or treatment. He expected to die.

I didn't have to be a rocket scientist to figure out that Gordon had now lost hope. He made it clear that he definitely would not try to obtain help from anyone, anymore. He didn't want to discuss the issue.

I tried to reason with him, saying that we should check into contacting our MP, MPP, ombudsman, or whoever, but Gordon told me he had already spoken with some government people and hadn't wanted to upset me by letting me know no hope existed there, either.

Some people suggested going out of country without medical coverage help, but truly that would have been an expensive proposition. Gordon didn't want to do this, for he felt that the cost would be prohibitive and he didn't want to burden us financially. He felt that if it broke the bank and treatment wasn't successful, I would be left to care for an out-of-country vegetable or left a widow to deal with the repercussions, both emotionally and financially.

Life definitely became harder. But, as long as Gordon lived, I still believed hope existed. After all, Jesus loved us. God would provide.

Chapter Seventeen

Hope

O nce back in Windsor, we tried to settle into a routine.
Gordon had an opportunity for an early retirement package from his employer. Without much discussion, we both were in agreement that he needed to do this.

Stress of any kind would set him off into the mood swings that I described in another chapter. I hoped that by removing some of the stress from Gordon's life, he would experience fewer of these moods and certainly cause less upset for him and for me.

Early retirement didn't really provide the type or amount of relief that I had hoped it would. Gordon's moods continued.

In addition, he emotionally gave up. He regularly spoke of God taking him home, to heaven.

Of course, his physical symptoms increased in both the type and intensity. New health concerns seemed to plague Gordon, on a regular basis. We spoke with his neurosurgeon with regards to this and received a referral to see another physician, a urologist. The medication Gordon received did absolutely nothing for him.

With regards to pain, I pleaded with Gordon's neurosurgeon to please help him. The specialist insisted no medication would alleviate the pain or the mood swings.

He reminded us that the problem was the location of Gordon's tumor. Had it been anywhere else, he might have been able to help.

In the very centre of his brain, the growth affected the area of hormone control. Every system in our body is run by hormones, whether digestion, heart, circulation, or any other major system.

Once again, the neurosurgeon reminded us that today the growth could affect one bodily function, while tomorrow it could affect another. Each system would need its own medications. Gordon could not be placed on multiple drugs at the same time. He insisted he could do nothing for him.

This did nothing to encourage Gordon—or me.

When we pleaded with him once again, regarding the mood swings, the neurosurgeon suggested Gordon see a psychiatrist, since they are the only other physicians who can administer drugs to someone with a brain problem as complicated as Gordon's.

Back we went to our family physician, to obtain a referral.

During the months of waiting for an appointment, Gordon's symptoms worsened. There were times when he didn't truly have control of himself. He did and said things totally out of character.

Going places, he would sometimes forget where he was going, or would forget how to get there.

His head pain increased, forcing him to spend more time in bed.

No matter what, I tried to remain positive, for both of us. Prayer, both at church, with friends, and with Gordon made up part of my regular routine.

In retrospect, I can see that I just could not seem to accept Gordon's real state of health. While it might be very normal for people to have trouble accepting a situation such as this, I knew that in my heart, I didn't because I kept on trusting that it *was* God's will to heal him.

Gordon arrived home many times by the assistance of neighbors living in our apartment building. Some were angry with me that he wandered on his own.

Of course, most people didn't understand that at the time when he left our apartment, he appeared to be okay, which also happened regularly, or I couldn't reason with him or physically constrain him, to keep him in our humble abode.

On one occasion, Gordon almost fell into the Detroit River. A woman saw him trip and fall onto the railing, where he tried to balance, being unable to once again get his feet onto the sidewalk. Not good.

This Good Samaritan rescued Gordon. When she brought him back to me, she made it clear that she wasn't happy; nor, was I.

As I've mentioned before, all Gordon's symptoms were intermittent. They came and went, without notice.

Eventually, Gordon stopped driving. We still had two vehicles for a while. He rode a bike when he felt he wanted some freedom or took a bus.

The change in his demeanor made a difference in how people reacted to him. There were times when his conduct got him into trouble.

Right before my eyes, he would change from a loving, kind-hearted soul, into someone I hardly recognized. Not just by the anger fits, but also with his speech and attitudes.

Eventually, after several months' wait, an appointment was arranged for Gordon to see another psychiatrist. We went to the same hospital, but this time to see a female doctor.

She spoke with both of us, taking notes, of course. Then, before we left, she asked me to keep track of information on Gordon's activities and moods.

We were both shocked with what she had to tell us regarding medications.

We were told that she diagnosed Gordon as having *Intermittent Explosive Disorder (IED)*, in addition to having the tumor in his brain.

While Wikipedia is not a medical authority, I liked the way it explained the disorder in layman terms. If you would like a more medically-oriented explanation, feel free to check it out for yourself.

Wikipedia explains *Intermittent Explosive Disorder* (IED) as the following:

"IED is a behavioral disorder characterized by extreme expressions of anger, often to the point of uncontrollable rage that are disproportionate to the situation at hand. It is currently categorized in the Diagnostic and Statistical Manual of Mental Disorders as an impulse control disorder. IED belongs to the larger family of Axis 1 impulse control disorders listed in the DSM-IV-TR, along with kleptomania, pyromania, pathological gambling, and others. Impulsive aggression is unpremeditated, and is defined by a disproportionate reaction to any provocation, real or perceived. Some individuals have reported affective changes prior to an outburst (e.g. tension, mood changes, energy changes, etc.)."

There is more to this article, but I am sure you can read it for yourself, if you are interested.

Gordon had *no control* over what happened to him; nor did I. His remorseful attitude after each episode was part of the disorder, for he truly could not control himself.

The psychiatrist explained that Gordon should never have any mild mood stabilizers and why Gordon's moods and anger worsened whenever our family physician treated him with drugs to relax him. Apparently, they could have the opposite effect, as we had observed.

Still, he received a prescription for a drug that this psychiatrist thought might help him. She admitted that she didn't know if this medication would work, because of his brain tumor situation.

When he first began his new medication, he seemed to be okay. Then, after a few days, he told me he felt sick. After about a week or so, he felt downright ill and itchy all over.

Recognizing that Gordon might have been allergic to the medication, we immediately saw the psychiatrist, again.

Instead of changing the medication, or taking him off it, she told Gordon it not to worry about a minor side-effect, such as this. She also increased the dosage.

For a few days, Gordon just stayed mainly in bed, feeling ill. Then, in the middle of the night, several days later, he woke me up, calling my name.

When I got up out of bed and went into the hallway, near our bathroom door, I couldn't believe my eyes. There Gordon stood, his face swollen and distorted, his lips at least three times or more their normal size.

Off we rushed to the hospital, to the emergency department, where we were grateful for the help Gordon so badly needed. Once in a bed, they administered an IV, giving him all the drugs they felt he needed to combat the allergic reaction Gordon had to the drug.

Unfortunately, the hospital couldn't reach the psychiatrist, due to her being away on holiday, out of the country. After treatment that took several hours, the ER physician directed Gordon to no longer take this drug and to seek further medical help from our normal physicians.

Back at home, Gordon left a message for the psychiatrist's office. No reply came, after several days, so he called, again. Same thing happened; no response.

Eventually, Gordon did receive a response to his final call to her office. He had wanted to make an appointment with his psychiatrist, but he never received one.

Instead, he received a letter notifying him that she was no longer seeing patients as she would be going into research.

Great! Once again, Gordon had no doctor and no help.

Back to our family physician's office we went. Once again, Gordon found himself placed on a waiting list of people needing a psychiatric doctor. He waited and waited.

Life, being difficult enough without this happening, once again felt like no hope could be found. Only this time, he was much worse off, physically.

In addition to Gordon being ill, without medical help or treatment, he grew more and more depressed.

By this time, I found myself being very discouraged and angry with our medical system, just like Gordon. How could this be happening? This system had been set up to give medical treatment to all who need it, so that no one would be left behind. Yet, somehow, Gordon fell through the cracks.

We believed that we, as taxpayers, were paying for this medical system that didn't allow for the only treatments we believed could help Gordon: Gamma Knife or Cyber Knife surgeries, Neither Gordon nor I believed that anyone should be able to fall through cracks of any kind. We believed that we had somehow lost control over our own health care.

Here we were again, facing *The Glass Wall*, with no way to access the only treatment we believed might help Gordon and no help to break through.

Believe me when I say I prayed more and more; harder and harder. I prayed for God's will to be to heal my husband, whom I loved more than my own life.

Even though we were both experiencing trauma in different ways, I believed God's will *was* to heal Gordon, even if he no longer believed it.

Chapter Eighteen

Things Get Worse

One day, one of our apartment neighbors came to my door. The police were across the street arresting Gordon. My heart took a leap, but I took a deep breath and asked what happened.

Apparently, the police had seen Gordon get a bottle of liquor out from the trunk of my vehicle parked there. He had been seen sitting down in the front seat, with the driver's door open and his legs on the ground, using the seat only as a place to sit, not to drive.

In retrospect, I can only believe someone *called* the police. Otherwise, if this had happened by chance that a police car saw Gordon sitting like this, drinking from a liquor bottle, there would have only been one police car.

But this didn't happen. *Two* police cars pulled into the parking area and surrounded my vehicle.

Even though the keys were not in the ignition, and even though he had not been fully seated in the vehicle and even though he no longer drove vehicles at all, the police charged Gordon with Driving Under the Influence (DUI).

It didn't make me happy to find out that Gordon had once again begun drinking. However, I also didn't feel it was right that he be arrested for something he hadn't done.

In any case, it cost us several thousand dollars to hire a lawyer and fight this, not to mention the stress it added to our lives. Stress that only served to bring on more episodes with Gordon, while making me feel like maybe God really wasn't there for us, after all.

In reality, I knew God *was* there for us, but my faith dwindled that He would heal Gordon.

Gordon's head pain had reached the point where he felt he *absolutely* needed something for pain and drugstore pain remedies did nothing to help, so he had recently begun drinking, again.

Be still my heart.

I immediately sold our second vehicle, so there would be one less hiding spot for Gordon to hide any alcohol and no further chance of a similar situation arising, again. We had been in the process of doing this, anyway. After all, without Gordon driving, why did we need two vehicles? I must admit that I hadn't rushed into selling the car due to believing Gordon would be healed and be able to drive, once again. This whole situation saddened me.

Because he could no longer go into a liquor store and purchase alcohol, Gordon stopped drinking. After all, once charged by police, there are rules the accused must abide by and this was one of them.

He once again attended AA meetings, sometimes by himself or sometimes with friends who lived in our apartment building who stepped forward out of their anonymity to help him.

Again, I began to praise God and thank Jesus for providing for us!

A happy camper didn't describe me, anymore. Not just with Gordon, because of what he had done, but also with the police, for how they treated my husband throughout this process. Please remember, I did not enable Gordon to drink. Nor was I happy with what he had done.

After all, years earlier, a driver ruined my life and got off virtually scot-free while my husband, being sick, mentally ill, and not in control of himself, wanting only to kill the pain he suffered with, had been arrested for drunk driving and would probably be convicted, even though he hadn't even driven the vehicle! Is this what they call being fair? I repeatedly asked myself *where's the justice in this*?

I had nowhere to turn, but to God. He provided for me. As always, he helped me deal with what I had been faced with.

Eventually, the charges were stayed, with the provision that Gordon not drink alcohol ever again.

When I say I noticed no difference with Gordon, whether he drank or not, I truly mean it.

When he had been drinking, he would pass out in bed and sleep for hours. When he had not been drinking, he would lie in bed awake or asleep for hours. At this point, I lived a life of virtual widowhood.

Things changed. He seemed to get worse, once again. In May of 2009, Gordon was hospitalized, anemic and losing blood.

As a result, we cancelled our plans to attend a family wedding in Northern Ireland, scheduled in July.

After being treated and discharged from hospital, Gordon reminded me of his desire to die; he just wanted God to take him home, to heaven.

Hearing this from the man I loved hurt me so very much that I can hardly even type it into this chapter. It still makes me cry.

By this time, Gordon had lost all hope of ever being healed. He felt like a living vegetable.

Evening after evening, I sat alone, in a widow-like state, praying with my whole being that it *was* God's will to heal Gordon. I never gave up, even though he had.

Then, something happened that I thought I never would ever have seen in my whole life.

I walked into my bedroom to speak with Gordon and instead of finding him lying in bed, I found him sitting up, chugalugging something.

The colored liquid in a water bottle resembled iced tea; I thought he had added a crystal mixture to his water. The telltale smell in the room gave it away. I smelled mouthwash.

I almost had heart-failure, right there on the spot.

Gordon told me that he truly couldn't stand the pain and needed something to knock him out.

I cried. I pleaded with God. I totally fell apart. I even lost my temper with Gordon.

The next day, I took him to the Canadian Mental Health Association. A worker there assessed Gordon and explained to me that for someone with Gordon's physical and emotional condition, this development was absolutely normal.

At first, I thought this woman had a screw loose. How could doing something like this be absolutely normal?

She explained that they regularly see cases where people who have medical conditions which have no treatment or medications available feel they need to self-medicate.

Hearing this did not make me feel any better. However, Gordon began attending a group meeting at CMHA. He was assigned a worker who could relate to the courts on his behalf, who met with him, regularly.

They also gave him a form to fill out, and to take to his doctor. This form was the one we needed in order to apply to our government, to have our medical system allow him to go out of country for medical treatment. However, it was explained to us this did not guarantee Gordon would be approved. Still, I looked at this as being good news. Things appeared to be looking up, at least for a short while.

After attending the CMHA group meeting for a couple of weeks, the group leader decided that Gordon's dilemma did not meet the criteria of the group and refused to allow him to participate any longer.

Things began to fall apart and I found him once again, drinking mouthwash.

The next day, I took him to dry out at the detox centre housed at a local hospital. Gordon voluntarily admitted himself and stayed about eight days, before being released.

He promised me that he did not want to return there. In an effort to prove himself to me, he asked me to take away from him his keys to our apartment, his wallet, money, identification, etc.

With Gordon's condition improved, we travelled to Kitchener where my younger brother was having surgery. We stayed at his apartment and used the time we weren't visiting at the hospital to clean things up for his return home.

Gordon had been a great help to me, even in his weakened and sickly state, considering he didn't really want to do anything but rest. Once we were done working on our last Sunday in Kichener, he stayed at the apartment alone while I went and had coffee with some family members. Afterwards, I went to visit my brother at his hospital room.

Returning, I was shocked to learn Gordon had been arrested. I rushed to the police station. Gordon had been drinking a bottle of mouthwash while walking through the complex's parking area, and a woman living there got nervous and called the police. When the officers searched Gordon's name, they found the conditions to his release from when the DUI charges had been stayed. So, they arrested him, thinking he had been drinking alcohol.

At the time we, just as the police had, assumed that the mouthwash contained alcohol, but it was only shown to me much later, that it indeed did not.

In any case, it was surprising to even me that I managed to stay calm with the police. The next day, I posted bail and was made to sign a legal document, making myself responsible for Gordon. Responsible to the point that if proven in court I neglected to report any knowledge I had of Gordon breaking the terms of his release, including drinking mouthwash, I would be arrested, convicted, and imprisoned. We hired a lawyer, once again.

On the way home every emotion possible washed over me. Anger, for sure, as well as distress as to what I should do, concerning Gordon. I cried almost the whole three hour trip. And due to Gordon's illness, I was doing all the driving.

No matter now repentant he seemed to be, it just didn't cut any ice with me. No matter how sorry he felt, it wouldn't affect the new problems that had arisen, or so it seemed.

Rather than raise my voice at Gordon, I cried out to God for help. I screamed at the top of my lungs, not at my husband, but to God. *Where are you?*

Gordon pleaded with me to not leave him. I assured him that when I made my vows before God, *for better or for worse*, I meant it. This could only be the *for worse*, once again.

I talked with Gordon about my fears of leaving him alone in our apartment. I spoke about my concern regarding him getting up in the middle of the night and leaving, as he had done at times, in the past. I felt I wouldn't be able to sleep.

No matter how hard I tried, I just could not work all this out in my mind. I actually thought I would lose it. My mind, I mean.

Gordon knew my legitimate concerns. After all, my future rested in the responsibility of the agreement I signed in that legal document, which placed me in the difficult position of having to report to the police if Gordon violated any term of condition for his release.

I couldn't stop crying.

Gordon insisted I take him once again to the detox centre; he needed to be in a safe environment. In addition, he believed this would give me time to calm down, relax somewhat before having to together make serious decisions.

Even though I had previously restored trust in Gordon enough to return to him his wallet and personal items before we began our trip to see my brother, he once again handed me his wallet, his keys, and all his personal items, other than his travel bag of clothing and books that we had brought to my brother's apartment.

For a second time, Gordon entered the detox program at the hospital. I went home, cried, and prayed to God for help.

Chapter Nineteen

Gordon's Last Month & Collapse…

Gordon stayed at the detox centre for about a week, once again. This time, he didn't have a positive state of mind, as before.

It broke my heart. All I did was cry for the first couple of days. I cried out to God, over and over, again. *Where are you? Why? Help!* Thoughts like those ran through my mind over and over. Whenever I could release some of the tension I carried, I would remind myself that I knew exactly where God was. He *was* with me. And, He *was* with Gordon.

A pastor friend had told me about *Teen Challenge*, a rehabilitation program for those with substance abuse problems. The program name is misleading, for it is not just for teens, but for people of all ages.

The closest location in Canada is in London, Ontario. And, it is a male only program, there.

I let Gordon know that I wanted him to enter the Teen Challenge rehab center, to participate in their one year live-in program. The thought did not thrill him. I encouraged him to consider it, because it was the *only* Christian program I had been able to locate within a day's driving distance from where we lived.

Gordon insisted he would rather attend a secular three month rehab program that he heard of closer to home. He didn't want to attend the long term program at Teen Challenge, because he didn't think he would live that long.

It had been the end of August at the time Gordon re-entered the detox centre. All throughout September, he suffered being violently ill. He did not drink…anything. No alcohol, no mouthwash. He also had nothing for pain that grew more unbearable for him, daily.

Even though Gordon suffered, I praised God and I thanked Jesus, because I didn't want to have to turn him in to the police had something gone wrong.

Nor did I want to find out he had been caught doing this again, knowing that if the police thought I knew about it and didn't report him, they would arrest me and I would face charges.

The head pain and illness Gordon continuously contended with, worsened. Even so, he went to Alcoholics Anonymous meetings and met with his worker from the Canadian Mental Health Association for coffee and conversation.

For at least the last two weeks before Gordon collapsed, he experienced such terrible head pain he could hardly function. He rarely left our bed and refused to eat regularly.

Even so, he told me his heart's desire was to visit Manitoulin Island, once again. He had been there many years before he met me and wanted to visit there, again.

We made plans leave home October 1, 2009 to drive through Michigan and visit friends in Grand Rapids, before making our way north, back to Canada and driving to Manitoulin Island.

Gordon was to meet with his CMHA worker in our lobby and go out for coffee the morning of our scheduled departure. Instead, he let his worker know that he just didn't feel well enough to go out of the building, even for a Tim Horton's coffee.

They stayed in our lobby and talked for a while.

Apparently, his pain was so intense he couldn't stand the sound of nearby people talking aloud. His worker later let me know that Gordon even moved his chair to another location, to cut down on the noise affecting his head.

Packed and ready to go, I thought we would leave as planned. But, when he told me of his extreme aching, our plans changed.

We decided that instead of leaving that day, we would allow Gordon to sleep and hopefully relax enough to feel improved. We would instead leave very early the next morning.

Insisting he didn't want to cancel, Gordon went to bed. I decided to go see my younger daughter for a while, so I left, but returned a short time later.

Gordon refused to eat supper. He just wanted to rest.

About ten p.m., I decided to get some sleep and climbed into bed, a short while later. Gordon got up to go to the washroom. He returned to our room, but after sitting on the side of our bed for just a moment, he once again went back to the bathroom.

Gordon hollered my name. He sounded in trouble, repeatedly calling for me. As I got up and made my way to help him, he began shaking our shower doors, saying I should let him in, because he couldn't get into our apartment.

Something was seriously wrong.

I helped Gordon. He wanted to return to bed, but I insisted he didn't.

Instead, I guided him into our living room and sat him down in his recliner chair. I told him I'd call for an ambulance, but he became angry and insisted I not call.

At the very least, he needed to go to the hospital, so I helped him get dressed and I once again got dressed. As I finished putting on my shoes, Gordon tried to get up from his chair.

He quickly sat down on the front edge of the seat, leaned forward and slid onto his knees on the floor. Telling me he was tired and just wanted to lie down until we were ready to leave, he lay down on the floor.

I called for an ambulance.

It took about twenty minutes or more for an ambulance to arrive. Gordon appeared to be breathing, so I thought he would be okay. Two ambulance attendants arrived, one being a strong-looking man, but the other being a thin, young woman. I was appalled, to say the least.

I asked if they were going to be able to lift and carry Gordon out of our apartment, into the hall where the gurney awaited. In my concern, I asked if I should immediately call for another ambulance.

The man told me to relax, that they were going to stabilize Gordon and set him up with an IV.

Once completed, he told me I needed to call for another ambulance. Talk about being angry! How dare they do this! I had asked them when they first arrived if I should do this.

I was also angry with myself, for in my heart of hearts, I knew I should have ignored what I had been told and immediately called for a second ambulance, because I doubted right from the beginning that they alone would be able to lift and carry my two hundred forty pound husband.

The second ambulance also took close to twenty minutes to arrive. It made me angry to see two thin, young women enter our home.

No, I didn't lose my temper, although I wanted to!

The three women and one man tried to lift Gordon. They finally managed to lift him, but couldn't carry him through the doorway.

So, I helped. Can you imagine?! A partially disabled wife having to assist four ambulance attendants who could not do the job that they had been called to do!

I asked that they take Gordon to the hospital where his neurosurgeon worked. It is about the same distance as the one they intended, but I thought it would be better for him to be treated where his specialist worked.

The male attendant told me they would take him there.

I had to take a separate elevator down to the lobby, where I met them, because with the gurney and attendants filling one elevator, there was no room for me. Then, one of the women attendants told me they were taking Gordon to the other hospital, not the one where his neurosurgeon worked. No matter how much I tried to reason with them, she insisted, claiming it would be closer.

I drove to the hospital, alone. Enroute, Gordon's ambulance passed me. I arrived just after midnight.

I was immediately ushered into a quiet room, where an emergency room doctor came to speak with me. He asked me if I wanted them to keep Gordon comfortable until he died, or if I wanted him treated.

I said, *"What?"* The ER physician explained to me that they believed my husband had been oxygen deprived for more than twenty minutes and would probably be a vegetable if he awoke, ever.

I asked what was wrong with Gordon. The ER physician said he didn't know. I replied that if they didn't have a diagnosis yet, then they should treat him.

Then, this doctor told me they would have to transfer Gordon to the same hospital I originally requested.

Off we both went to the other hospital; Gordon by ambulance, me in my van.

He was immediately taken to the ICU. After three a.m., I finally got to see him.

In the meantime, a hospital chaplain came to see me. Actually, I had met her on a previous occasion years earlier, when she prayed with me and Gordon's mom. This Salvation Army chaplain proved to be a true blessing to me. She arranged a quiet room immediately beside the entrance to ICU, designated for me alone. Family and friends could join me there, but I was grateful I was able to lie down there to rest. Or, pray.

I did a lot of that. Pray, I mean.

Friends and my younger daughter came to support me. They visited Gordon and prayed for him, with me.

Our pastor and elders from our church came. They laid hands on Gordon, anointed him with oil, and prayed for him, as the Bible directs.

At first, the staff allowed to see Gordon and spend time with him any time I wanted to, as long as the medical staff didn't need to be alone with him. I was grateful!

I sang quietly in his ear. I prayed aloud over him. I prayed silently. I wrote on the palm of Gordon's hand the way he had done for me, whenever I had been in hospital for surgeries.

I wrote: *Jesus loves you and so do I! Love, Lynnie.*

Then, things began to change.

The floor physician caring for Gordon and a nurse talked with me, asking me to allow them to unplug Gordon's life support. I refused.

Every day, they badgered me to do this. They claimed that he would be a vegetable if he awoke. I believed God would provide a miracle.

Most people there didn't believe in miracles, but I had seen God do one, before. No. I'm not referring to the miracle God provided for my daughter during the bus collision.

God had provided a miracle for my elder daughter's second son, when he had been about six weeks premature.

The neonatologist who cared for my grandson was Christian. He found out my daughter was Christian and asked her if he could bring in his pastor and elders from his church, lay hands and anoint my grandson with oil while praying over him. My daughter agreed.

What a blessing my daughter received, finding out just prior to his being released from hospital, that my grandson's original scan had showed brain damage, but the scan done just prior to his discharge showed no brain damage. His specialist made it clear to my daughter that she and her son had received a miracle from God.

He explained that brain damage does not go away; it doesn't just disappear. There is no treatment or cure. He made it clear to my daughter that my grandson did not become healed by anything he or the nursing staff had done. Plain and simple, it *was* God's doing.

So, every time Gordon's medical staff approached me, they reiterated the idea that if I didn't agree to remove him from life support, I risked him waking up in a vegetative state.

I made it clear to all that I believed God would provide a miracle and refused to participate in Gordon's death.

Another neurologist had a CT scan done of Gordon's brain.

He, along with the floor physician and some nurses, showed me Gordon's brain CT scan. Without something to compare it to, I couldn't see what they were trying to convince me of.

They told me the marks in his brain were brain damage. I asked if it could be swelling. The neurologist replied," *Yes, it could be swelling.*"

Upon hearing it could be what I enquired of, I refused to agree to unplug my husband. I truly believed God would perform yet another miracle in our lives. And, I told them this.

Then, things worsened. They began to refuse to allow me to see my husband, even during visiting hours. I was told it was due to the fact that medical staff needed time with him.

Visitors can attest that time after time, I would ring the buzzer and be refused entrance.

I became angry. But, instead of expressing my anger, I prayed for all involved.

The floor manager had a private meeting with me. He claimed to be Christian and explained that in everyone's best interest, I should agree to allow Gordon's life to be ended. While being very pleasant and listening to my concerns and complaints, in the end, it was meaningless and of no value, at all.

Please realize, Gordon *was not* brain dead. In fact, his general condition improved as time went on. This only increased their concern, for they believed that if Gordon was allowed to wake up, he would wake up a vegetable, unable to care for himself, requiring much care and medical treatment.

My daughter, whose son has a heart condition, understood all the equipment they were using on Gordon. She told me that whenever I gave Gordon my attention, touching him and talking to him, kissing him, or whatever, his numbers began stabilizing. Once she pointed this out to me, I could see it, myself.

When I made this very point to the medical staff, they agreed. They recognized it, too. Still, day after day, I was subjected to this harassment of ending Gordon's life.

In their opinion, Gordon could die a peaceful death, if I just allowed them to unplug him.

Nope. I had no intention of participating in ending my husband's life. I repeatedly asked them if Gordon could die even though life support kept him alive. They replied, repeatedly, that he could. In my opinion, their answer supported my belief.

Gordon would only be taken home to heaven to be with Jesus if God willed it. At least, this is what would happen if I had my way. It didn't quite work out the way I thought it would.

On the eighth of October, and while still having serious problems with the hospital staff not always allowing me in to be with my husband, the hospital staff let me know that they did not want me staying overnight in the quiet room and insisted I go home to sleep.

So, I did.

In the middle of the night, my telephone rang. It was the hospital.

His nurse let me know Gordon was in crisis. She told me to bring everyone who might want to see him before he died and get there as soon as possible.

I called Gordon's family and my younger daughter. We met at the hospital, to find that Gordon was no longer in crisis by the time we arrived. In fact, he seemed to be stable as like other times we visited.

However, I noticed that they had removed some of Gordon's life support equipment, so he had less tubes, etc. surrounding him. Staff told me he no longer needed some of it.

However, we were also notified of a meeting planned for us to meet with Gordon's floor physician, the floor supervisor and some nursing staff. They required us all to be there.

In my heart, I knew this meeting wasn't going to be good. My heart broke for Gordon. I prayed for him and for me, for I knew I needed strength that could only come from my Lord.

Chapter Twenty

Gordon's Last Day

Together, my daughter, one of Gordon's family members, and I met with the medical staff.

Gordon's floor physician did most of the talking. She let us know that the decision to pull Gordon's plug and end his life had been taken out of my hands.

Forgive me, but my first thought *was not* of Gordon. Rather, my first thought was, *are we living in Nazi Germany, like during WW2?* What happened to us being in control of our own healthcare?

We were also told that later that same day, October ninth, the hospital would proceed removing all Gordon's life support. The decision had been made by hospital officials. No recourse was available; nothing I or anyone else could do or say would make any difference. Their minds were made up. Nothing could make enough difference to change the course ahead, for only a court order would make a difference and I knew there wasn't time to obtain this.

I knew this from a past experience Gordon and I had endured. During this horrifying past experience, he and I had called the police and several lawyers in an effort to stop what was happening to a loved one, but were told it was too late, that we would not be able to change the future for the person.

So, here I sat, horrified once again, knowing in my heart that I could *nothing* for my husband.

I looked to God to help me. I told myself that God's will is always done. At least I had a clear conscience, knowing I had done everything I possibly could for Gordon. If he were to die, it would be at someone else's hands. Not mine.

We were told they weren't going to be cruel about it, but we should bring anyone we thought would want to say good-bye to him before four p.m., the time they had scheduled for him to be removed fully from life support.

Gordon's relative said good-bye, immediately; he didn't want to be there when Gordon died.

My daughter and I stayed.

After the medical staff left, we were joined in the meeting room by people representing the transplant team.

Gordon had been a registered organ donor. So, this team explained to us that they wanted to use my husband's kidneys.

I let them know that both my brothers, plus another friend, were dialysis patients in the Kitchener/Guelph/Cambridge areas. I also requested they determine if Gordon would be a match for any of them.

They informed me he wasn't a match for our family or friend, because his rare blood type didn't match theirs.

The extensive paperwork took a long time, for the team had to explain everything involved with regards to transplants.

They explained to us that we should ignore what the hospital staff had told us with regards to Gordon being unplugged about four p.m. His life support would not be removed before this time, but more was explained.

Apparently, from their point of view, Gordon would remain on life support until at least that time, but would not be unplugged until a transport team could arrive from London, Ontario, about a two hour drive away from our city. They had to be in place, ready to roll as soon as Gordon's kidneys had been removed.

It took all my strength to not fall apart. I prayed my God would help me through this process.

I prayed *Help me, Lord!* I knew I couldn't do this without God lifting me up and carrying me.

We got in touch with another of Gordon's relatives at work. Later in the day, she came and joined us at the hospital. In the afternoon, our pastor joined us, also.

However, during the afternoon, we were once again refused entry to visit with Gordon, even though it definitely was his last few hours of life.

Some of my friends who sat with me at the hospital were as disgusted as me. I actually felt rage.

How dare they keep me from my husband? It sickened my heart that they planned to force his death by about four o'clock or shortly after.

We were allowed in to see him, only for a short time, after complaining.

Then, once again, they allowed no one to see him for a while.

About six p.m. and feeling really angry, I did exactly as my friend suggested. They suggested just entering ICU, when visitors for other people were entering. In my daughter and I went!

Gordon's nurse did not want us to stay. This is when I truly lost it!

I let her know how angry I was over them not allowing me to spend time with my husband on his last day on earth. I recall asking her if she would be happy if our roles were reversed, if I were in her shoes and she in mine. Wouldn't she *want* to be with her husband, especially since he would only be alive for a short time, a few hours at the most?

I told her that I prayed she would never be faced with what I was going through, and the painfulness of the situation.

She relented and allowed us to remain with Gordon. When I calmed down, I apologized to her.

Every time the transplant team came into Gordon's area, my heart skipped a beat. I knew that one of those times they would be notifying me that the transport team had arrived and they would be taking Gordon away from me, forever.

But, time after time, they kept telling me about some sort of delay. I kept praying God would help me through this heartbreaking trial.

Then about eleven forty-five p.m., the transplant team arrived, letting me know that the London, Ontario transport team would not be able to come to Windsor, to pick up Gordon's kidneys. They told me that because of Gordon's rare blood type, a Toronto, Ontario hospital wanted them and were prepared to send an airplane to pick them up.

However, they claimed that as they were doing one final check before the plane would depart, they found that Gordon's kidneys were beginning to fail. They confirmed that this meant a plane would not be coming.

They then notified us that at midnight, Gordon's nurse would begin a morphine IV, to ensure Gordon wouldn't have pain when they removed the remaining life support at approximately twelve fifteen a.m.

That is exactly what they did.

After Gordon's life support was fully removed, I watched his color drain from his face. Eventually, he became gray, and I knew he was gone.

The hospital pronounced Gordon dead at twelve-thirty a.m.

Gordon's relative, my younger daughter, and I left the hospital, about twelve forty-five a.m. October 10, 2009. We all went our separate ways, with each of the two young people going to be with their families.

I went home, alone.

Well, I truly wasn't alone, for God was with me.

Chapter Twenty-One

Refiner's Fire

Have you ever sung the song, *Refiner's Fire*? I have. Probably, you have, too. Did you mean it, when you sang it? If so, you prayed for God to purify your heart, cleanse you and make you holy.

Everything we sing to our Lord is as a prayer. If you didn't mean it and sang those lyrics, you might not be happy with the outcome. For God takes seriously what we pray.

No, He's not a genie in a bottle. He doesn't grant every wish or prayer that we ask of Him. And, praise God for that! I can look back at my life and see when I asked Him for something, that, later, I was glad I didn't receive.

However, it doesn't change the fact that God purifies those who belong to Him. Once we are saved and become His children, we can be sure that God will fulfill one of the promises He made us.

In Romans 8, one of my favorite chapters in the Bible, God told us in verses 29-31, *"For whom He foreknew, He also predestined to be conformed to the image of His Son, that He might be the firstborn among many brethren. Moreover whom He predestined, these He also called; whom He called, these He also justified; and whom He justified, these He also glorified. What shall we say to these things? If God is for us, who can be against us?"*

God is definitely for us, His children. God did not spare His own Son, but delivered Him up for us all (*Romans 8:32*). He told us in John 3:16, *"For God so loved the world, that He gave His only begotten Son, that whosoever believeth on Him should not perish, but have everlasting life."*

Think about this for a moment. What did *you* do to deserve God making a plan of salvation for you, before you were even born?

All we have to do is trust in Jesus or believe upon Him and we shall be saved (*Acts 16:31*). How can salvation be simpler?

Jesus loves you and me. He loved us so much that while we were yet sinners, Christ died for us (*Romans 5:8*).

Who else do you know that would die for you? Would your parents, spouse, or maybe other family members? Would a good friend? Only God knows. But, Jesus did. He fulfilled God's plan. He died for the sins of all who believe upon Him.

God made this simple plan so that you and I could be made righteous. You see, God cannot look upon sin. He cannot; period.

And His Word tells us that all have sinned and fallen short of the glory of God (*Romans 3:23*). That's you and me; sinners. We've all fallen short. No one is perfect; no one, but our Savior, Jesus Christ.

Through His shed blood on Calvary, He covers our sin, so that God the Father cannot see it. We are made righteous through Jesus.

However, salvation is not the end of our relationship with God. It's truly just the beginning, for as you read earlier, His will is to conform us, His children, into the image of His Son, Jesus Christ.

How does God do this?

Well, think of it this way. God is the Potter and we are the clay. In order for a potter to mold clay, he must first mix the clay. Once he has clay to work with, he must literally work the clay, sort of like how a baker would knead bread dough. After much kneading, pushing, pulling, punching, the clay becomes workable. It breaks down to the point where it can be used for the purpose of molding.

Once He has finished making the clay pliable enough to be used by him, he forms the clay into the vessel he is creating. After the shape has been determined, he places the vessel into a kiln, where the fire refines the clay. The heat builds and once again converts the clay from a soft mass into a vessel strong enough to be used for the intended purpose.

Have you ever felt broken? Have you ever felt like you were being beaten up, emotionally? Like you've walked through fire? Like me, I'm sure you have.

I have written about some of the trials in my life, not to complain or whine about having hurt a lot in my life. Rather, I have written about *a few* of the trials in my life, so you can see you are not alone. You can understand that I truly have experienced pain and suffering, as you probably have.

In fact, I've experienced many more trials, with some being even more serious or worse than some I have told you about, here.

At this point, I want to let you know that when writing about some of my life's trials, I did not mean to hurt anyone, in any way. Nor, was I trying to not honor my parents, for I do honor them. I am proud of the people they were, even if we did have our share of life problems. It's true they weren't perfect people, but then, who is?

Had my intention in writing, been only to be self-serving in the context of trying to let the world know of the pain and heartache I've experienced in life, I would have written about trials even *more* heart-breaking to me. I would have discussed some issues in more depth, revealing the gut-wrenching pain I suffered relating to those circumstances. Yes, believe it or not, some of the pain I experienced relating to what I have elected to discuss here, wasn't even revealed.

What I chose to include for you to know about some of my life's trials, has been to serve as an illustration of not just how I have been through the refining fire, but also about God's goodness in bringing me through. Just as He brought me through, He will bring you through your pain and suffering.

My intention in explaining some heartbreaks of my life is so you can see that you are not alone. If you couldn't read about my selected trials, how could you understand?

Everyone has trials in their lives. While some testing is more serious than others, one fact is evident. We all experience tribulation.

In 1 Peter 4:12-13, God says to us, "*Beloved think it not strange concerning the fiery trial which is to try you, as though some strange thing happened unto you: But rejoice, inasmuch as ye are partakers of Christ's sufferings; that, when His glory shall be revealed, ye may be glad also wit exceeding joy.*"

God told us that the rain will fall on the just and on the unjust (*Matthew 5:45*). This means that whether we are saved or not saved, all people will have troubles or trials in their lives. We cannot escape them. It's part of God's plan.

Remember though, that part of His plan is for His children to be conformed into the image of His Son. His Son, Jesus Christ, who is perfect. How can we be made perfect, if God does not work us and mold us?

It is these very trials of life that we hate so much to experience, that God uses to mold us into the people He wants us to be. As we experience these trials, He develops our character, so we can be all He wants us to be.

In retrospect, I can honestly say I must have needed a lot of molding! That may sound like I'm joking, but I truly am not.

God knows the end from the beginning (*Isaiah 46:10*). He alone knows the plans He has for us, plans to help us and not harm us, to give us hope and a future (*Jeremiah 29:11*).

While God gives us free will, to make choices in life, He already knows what those choices will be. And, still He loves us.

Why? Love never fails.

Chapter Twenty-Two

Faith, Hope and Charity (Love)

W ithout faith, we are nothing. I say this, because without faith, it is impossible to please God (*Hebrews 11:6*). Pleasing God is *everything*.

He didn't save us so that we could just throw our lives away. He expects obedience from us, now that He has saved us from an eternity in hell.

As a child, I came to know Jesus. I loved Him. But, like so many before me and since, I fell away.

While my family considered themselves being of a Christian denomination, they did not consider themselves born-again Christians. Nor, did they read the Bible, or teach us children from God's Word.

We moved a lot. Not all were short moves, but some were truly long-distance moves.

Every time we moved, we either began worship at not just another church, but usually another denomination, as well. In some cases, we didn't attend church, at all.

I cannot say I am a perfect person, for I am not. However, in my younger years, I did not have the relationship with my Lord and Savior, Jesus Christ that I have, today.

Today, Jesus is everything to me. God is the most important part of my life. I truly live for Him. I have come to realize that *He is in control*, not me.

He provides for all my needs, not me. He may use people, places, and things, or instances and situations to provide for my needs, but He truly does *all* the providing. I can do nothing, without Him. I cannot even take my next breath, without God ordaining it. Neither can you.

While living through some of the deepest, darkest trials and times of my life, I somehow knew God was there for me; even when I was out of fellowship, with sin in my life.

Yes, I am a sinner. I recognize that my sin began with Adam and Eve, in the Garden of Eden and accept the fact that I have inherited sin.

In my life, I have made some poor choices. Like many of you. Some of those choices led to trials in my life, because of sin. However, not all the trials in my life were caused by my choices. God alone determines if He will rebuke us for those poor choices, or whether or not He will allow trials in our lives in order to build character in us and mold us into the people He wants us to be.

As I said in the last chapter, I must have needed a lot of molding! Even so, my faith has brought me to a place where I can see God has always been working in my life.

He has done the same for you, friend. If you have experienced trials in your life, it is *not* because God doesn't love you.

Those trials did not occur because you were rejected by God. God told us in Hebrews 12:6, *"For whom the Lord loveth he chasteneth, and scourgeth every son whom he receiveth."*

In other words, because God loves us, He disciplines us, rebukes us, and cleans us up. He loves us, just as you love your children. He wants only the best for us.

He wants only the best for *you.*

Can you see where God has been as you suffered in your trials of life? Wasn't He truly there for you? Didn't He lift you up and encourage you? Didn't He ultimately provide for you? Didn't you make it through the trial?

Of course He did. He did this for me and for you. We just need to recognize this truth.

Many times, I felt truly alone, in the midst of any one of my trials. Years ago, I had no idea why I experienced trial after trial, after trial. Today, I understand better and I hope you do, too.

I used to feel like a female Job; sometimes, I still do. As a child of God, I hope you have read the book of Job in the Old Testament, but if you are a new believer, you may not yet have done so. If not, I suggest you read it.

As you read how God loved Job and how Job suffered through the many trials of his life, you will probably feel you can relate, just as I do. Let's face it; it's not easy living through those times when you feel like your life has totally fallen apart. When you feel like giving up.

Job didn't give up, though. He had great faith. He stood firm in his conviction that God was for him and never waivered. I wish I could say I had always been that strong in my faith.

However, God *did* love Job. Once the trial ended, God restored Job's life. That, my friend, is love.

God didn't have to do this. Restoration is something we all dream of in this life. God did it for Job. I believe He is doing this for me at the moment, and I trust that He will do it for you, also.

While my life has not yet been totally restored, I believe that God is providing a measure of restoration and will continue to do so for me, as I am obedient to Him. I also believe He will do this for you, too.

Our hope is in the Lord, who gave Himself for us. He promised He would never leave us, nor forsake us, that He'd be with us always, even to the end of the age.

After all, God did tell us in Matthew 6:33, *"But seek ye first the kingdom of God and His righteousness; and all these things shall be added unto you."* God wants us to put Him first in our lives; then, He will provide for everything in our life. Wow! Double wow!

When we put God first in our lives, we are showing Him our love for *Him.* By sending His only begotten Son to earth to die on a wooden cross for the sin of all who would believe in Him, God showed us His love for us. Jesus showed us His love. Now, it is our turn to show our love.

So, keep the faith, friend. Our hope is in the Lord. Why? Because love never fails.

Chapter Twenty-Three

Love Never Fails You

The purpose of my writing this book is to help those of you who are going through heart-breaking trials or grief to understand that even though you may feel forgotten, *you are not.*

God has not forgotten you.

God loves you, friend. He provides for your every need. Sometimes, even for your greed, but not always.

Life isn't easy. Not for me and not for you. It wasn't meant to be. God didn't promise us an easy life.

I must say that if you are not yet saved, please consider coming to Christ, today. Salvation is of utmost importance. Without it, you will spend eternity in hell, separated from God, with no chance of escape.

Jesus Christ is not only the *only* way to God, the truth and the life (*John 14:6*), but he is our Savior, who truly loves His own.

Not only did God make a way of escape from hell for you, He also promised to never leave you, nor forsake you and to be with you always, even 'til the end of the age.

In retrospect, right from the first time I came to know and love Jesus, I knew He loved me. Even at those times when as a child, I felt I lived an awful life, I knew God loved me.

As a teenager, experiencing trials that brought separation with my family, I knew God never left my side. He provided for me, always.

Even when I didn't always look to Him, He was there with me, girding me up. Just as He is with you right now, and has been throughout your trials. He's there for you, because He loves you.

When my first marriage fell apart, God was there with me. I may not have always been there with Him, but somehow I always knew He never left me.

The proof of this being true was when the truck hit my bus. I may have been trusting in Jesus at that time, but I certainly hadn't been walking with Him, in fellowship. I hardly went to worship my God, nor did I focus on Him at that time. Yet, He loved me and my daughter enough to provide a modern day miracle and save her from certain physical death.

Thank You, Lord! I praise God and thank Jesus for the testimony He gave us, to His goodness, love and mercy for us.

Even with such a hard time recovering from the collision, enduring health problems, undergoing several surgeries and other life's trials, God always provided for me. Why? Only God knows, but I say with all conviction, that we are still here, because God had a plan for us.

I praise God that He never walked away from me, even when I had sin in my life.

Let's face it, no one is perfect. Each of us, from time to time have sin in our lives, particularly if we have not yet developed a personal relationship with Jesus. Hopefully, you'll agree with that statement, if you are truly honest with yourself.

Even when I thought both Gordon and I were truly being blessed, being married to each other, and finding out that God's plan didn't include a lifetime of happiness together, but rather a shorter version of a lifetime, with death forthcoming, I knew God was with me.

Living through the trial of dealing with not just the heartbreak of Gordon's ill health, but also dealing with the additional trials that occurred as a result of his ill health, certainly proved difficult. Still I knew God was with me; and, with Gordon.

When Gordon's emotional state deteriorated and his memory failed, God was with us. He provided, always.

When my husband became hospitalized, the evil one tried to deter me from trusting in my Lord, but he failed. God was with me, telling me everything would be okay.

When Gordon's final day came and life for me measured an ultimate low, God was there with me, girding me up, providing for me. I could not have made it through that time, without Him.

Grief hasn't been easy. Even with attending a local Christian church for grief counseling, it has been hard. While in my heart I knew that God had not abandoned me, I seemed to feel very alone. I cried out to God, regularly.

While I have grieved the loss of parents, grandparents, friends, and even a brother, nothing has compared to the loss I feel over losing my husband. It is hard to lose someone who truly loves you.

Whatever the case, dealing with grief over losing my spouse has been the worst. In the beginning, it surprised me that I could even breathe. To be honest, if I had stopped breathing, I would have been very happy, for then I would have been with my Lord and with my husband.

Night after night, I prayed it was God's will to allow me to fall asleep, as sleep evaded me. I prayed that after finally falling asleep, it was God's will to not allow me to wake up in the morning, here on earth. I dreamed, desired and prayed of God just taking me home, with Him.

Night after night, I cried. God tells us that He collects all our tears in a bottle; I recall telling a friend one day, that I believed God needed a whole ocean for mine, for a bottle wouldn't have been large enough!

The pain, suffering, and sorrow felt so great that I can recall on many occasions being out driving in my van and literally screaming out to God! Notice I didn't say I screamed *at* God, but rather *to* God, "*Where are You?*" I felt abandoned and alone. But, in my heart, I knew He hadn't left me.

It is safe to say that I don't know if I will ever stop grieving the loss of my husband, Gordon. I truly loved him; and, still do. Knowing that I have friends who are still grieving after many a year, I realize that grief doesn't ever really end. It seems people just adapt to a new life as time goes by.

I will go so far as to say that grieving the loss of Gordon and dealing with everything I went through with him has been the hardest trial of my life. Of course, when we are in the midst of a trial or are grieving a loss of any kind in our lives, we always feel like that particular trial or loss is the worst one we have experienced. At least, that's the way it has been, for me.

God provides for me, daily. He provides for you, too. He said He takes care of the birds of the air and the lilies of the field and aren't we even more important than they are (*Matthew 6:26*). God made those promises to me...and to you, if you are His child.

For those experiencing trials or grief at this time, my prayer is that you will read your Bible, God's Word, and memorize scriptures for yourself. When you find God's promises he made to us, highlight them and memorize them. It truly is a blessing to be able to recall one or more, at a moment in time when all feels lost.

Even though we may not know each other in a real life, physical sense, please know that I pray for you. I pray for all my brothers and sisters in the Lord who are experiencing trials and/or grief.

God never promised us a rose garden, but he sure has provided relief from the pain that thorns cause.

I truly love the whole chapter of Romans 8.

God begins that chapter by telling us that, "*There is no condemnation to those who are in Christ Jesus, who do not walk according to the flesh, but according to the Spirit. For the law of he Spirit of life in Christ Jesus has made me free from the law of sin and death.*"

We are reminded in verses 5 through 8, that to be walking in the flesh, being carnally minded is death, but to be spiritually minded is life and peace; that those who are in the flesh cannot please God.

For if we are not in the flesh, and if the Spirit of God dwells in us and if Christ is in us, our bodies are dead to sin (*verses 9-13*). Verse 14 tells us, *"For as many as are led by the Spirit of God, these are sons of God."*

We are told in verses 16 to 17 that, *"The Spirit Himself bears witness we are children of God, and if children, then heirs—heirs of God and joint heirs with Christ, if indeed we suffer with Him, that we may also be glorified."*

Isn't this amazing?! There is no condemnation to us, who are God's children! God has promised to glorify those of us who suffer with Christ!

What consolation this has been to me, throughout my deeper relationship with my Lord! I praise God and thank Jesus for everything in my life, both the good and the not so good.

In verse 26, God tells us that the Spirit also helps in our weaknesses and makes intercession for us. Praise God! Thank you, Jesus!

And then, in verse 28, we read one of God's great promises to us, *"And we know that all things work together for good to those who love God, to those who are the called according to His purpose."*

Notice that *God didn't say all things are good*. We know all things aren't.

However, we are assured that God will use all things in our lives, whether good or not so good, to bring about some eventual good.

As we discussed earlier, verses 29-31 tell us another reality of God, that He knew us, predestined us to be conformed to the image of His son; that He called us, justified us, and glorified us, reminding us that if God is for us, who can be against us?!

Each of us needs to look at our trials through God's eyes.

While we cannot always understand why we suffer through various trials in our lives, we are assured that we experience those trials, because those who belong to God were destined to be transformed into the image of His Son, our Lord Jesus Christ!

After all, God did not spare His own Son from pain and suffering, did He? Verse 29 confirms this.

"We are accounted as sheep for the slaughter," verse 36 tells us, but the promise continues in verse 37, *"Yet in all these things we are more than conquerors through Him who loved us."*

God has not left us to fall into trials, alone. In addition to Christian friends who lift us up, He has provided *all* things for us, even promising that we can conquer all things through Christ, who loves us.

He expects to receive our love, too. Jesus said in John 14:15, *"If ye love me, keep my commandments."* When we love God in return, He is glorified.

That assurance of never being alone again without God, comes in verses 38-39, *"For I am persuaded that neither death nor life, nor angels nor principalities nor powers, nor things present nor things to come, nor height nor depth, nor any other created thing, shall be able to separate us from the love of God which is in Christ Jesus our Lord."*

What a promise! How could we ever have a promise greater than this?

God has promised us that no matter what trial we go through in life, He is with us, always. Nothing will ever be able to separate us from Him!

Sometimes, when I think of God's promises, I become overwhelmed. There are times when tears running down my face are tears of joy and not of sadness.

Just thinking how God made a plan for me, and for you, to not only come to Him, but also to promise us that nothing can ever separate us from Him, is almost too much to comprehend!

Why would God love us, His children? Only God knows; just as He alone knows why He chose us before time to be part of His family. He told us in Romans 9:15, *"I will have mercy on whomever I will have mercy, and I will have compassion on whomever I will have compassion."*

It's God's plan. Who are we to question God? I believe we must be grateful for all God has provided for us, even through our tears.

He created His plan for my life and for your life, including every trial each of us will ever experience, because He loves us. God wants us to cast all our care upon Him, for He cares for us (*1 Peter 5:7*).

Another favorite chapter of mine is 1 Corinthians 13.

God tells us in verses 1-3, *"Though I speak with the tongues of men and of angels, but have not love, I have become sounding brass or a clanging cymbal. And though I have the gift of prophecy, and understand all mysteries and all knowledge, and though I have all faith, so that I could remove mountains, but have not love, I am nothing."*

This chapter of love shows us that love is more important than anything else.

I can totally relate to verses 4-7, *"Love suffers long and is kind; love does not envy; love does not parade itself, is not puffed up; does not behave rudely, does not seek its own, is not provoked, thinks no evil; does not rejoice in iniquity, but rejoices in the truth; bears all things, believes all things, hopes all things, endures all things."*

Why? Because, *"Love never fails."* as we are told in verse 8. *Love never fails.*

After I had been injured or required surgery, it would have been simple for Gordon to have just walked away from me. But, he didn't. Instead, Gordon loved me. He took care of me, and loved me through all the physical and emotional trials I experienced.

When Gordon fell ill, I held firm to my faith, regarding love; the true love, not just my love for him, but also of God

It wasn't easy dealing with life's trials during the time of Gordon's illness that led up to his death. Yet, they were both with me. Both Gordon and God loved me. And, I loved them.

When Gordon's mental condition deteriorated, I cannot tell you how many times a couple of close friends, who were the only people who knew and understood the true situation, offered me refuge. On a couple of occasions, when he seemed totally out of control, I can recall it even being suggested that I needed to leave him, for my safety, alone.

Did I do this? No. Instead, I trusted God that it wasn't His plan for me to be physically hurt or worse, by my husband, at those times when he could not control himself.

I trusted God. Just as you need to trust God, now; especially when you are experiencing a trial of life, or grief over losing someone you love.

We know that God does not *cause* trials in our lives. He may *allow* them, for our ultimate benefit, to help mold us into the people He wants us to be, but we don't always understand.

God told us in verse 12, "*For now we see in a mirror, dimly, but then face to face. Now I know in part, but then I shall know just as I also am known.*" Eventually, when we are in heaven with Him, we will know all things. God promised us this.

But, the best God saved for last, in verse 13, where He tells us, "*And now abide faith, hope, love, these three; but the greatest of these is love.*"

Always remember, "*He that loveth not knoweth not God; for God is love.*" (1 John 4:8). Love never failed me. And, *love never fails you.*

CPSIA information can be obtained at www.ICGtesting.com
Printed in the USA
LVOW122012220612

287284LV00015B/8/P